COOK BOOK
BY MARTIN WISHART

PHOTOGRAPHS BY ALAN DONALDSON

Dedicated to Cecile, Clara and Amy - **enjoy!**

PUBLISHING DIRECTOR: Martin Wishart

CREATIVE DIRECTOR: Peter McDermott PHOTOGRAPHER: Alan Donaldson

TEXT: Martin Wishart Scott Ross Fiona Armstrong

First published in 2008 by Mr Max Publishing
54 The Shore, Edinburgh EH6 6RA

Cataloguing in Publication Data: a catalogue record for this book is available from the British Library.

ISBN-10: 0-9559046-0-9
ISBN-13: 978-0-9559046-0-8

Printed in Italy by Graphicom

"Enjoy walking through the door of your own restaurant for the first time: it's only going to happen to you once."

using the recipes...

Many of the recipes in this book use basic stocks and sauces as part of their ingredients. The recipes for these basics are contained within their own section at the back of this book and are numbered *1* to *29*.
When a recipe requires the use of one of these basic recipes the following instruction will appear - *see basic 3*

All spoon measures are level unless otherwise stated:
1 teaspoon = 5ml spoon; 1 tablespoon = 15ml spoon.

To achieve the best results it is recommended to use the finest and freshest ingredients possible. Cooking times may vary due to different oven performances.

contents

Gavroche

foreword

I REMEMBER THE AUTUMN of 1991 for many reasons, the one that strikes me the most is that after much reflection and time already spent in the kitchens of Le Gavroche, I finally took over the full time running of the business from my father Albert. It was also the time that a young Scottish chef, still wet behind the ears, pushed the swing doors that lead into the training ground that is called Le Gavroche kitchens. Martin like so many young eager chefs wanted to learn what is in my view essential to become a great chef, and that is what is called French Classical Cuisine. Work in the kitchens is notoriously hard and this one is if anything harder still. But another attribute needed to be a great chef is perseverance and Martin certainly has that. His duties when he started were the most menial vegetable preparation, however through his ability to learn quickly and dedication to his profession, he was soon promoted to other sections of this frenetic school of hard knocks kitchen in Mayfair. He left us enriched and with classic training under his belt.

The time spent at Le Gavroche opened many doors to future employment and he even came back to the Roux family as a Sous-Chef at the Grand Hotel Amsterdam where my father was a consultant. It gives me enormous satisfaction and pride when a Gavroche old boy such as Martin fulfils their dreams and is successful; he is a real chef, with not only a natural talent, but a fundamental understanding of taste and gastronomy. *Michel Roux*

B. Onions
peas & feves

"I love being around food."

IT WAS A COLD, CRISP FEBRUARY MORNING in 1999 when I first collected the keys to what's now Restaurant Martin Wishart in Leith, Edinburgh. My Dad advised me to savour what was one of the most exciting moments of my life: *"Enjoy walking through the door of your own restaurant for the first time: it's only going to happen to you once."*

For as long as I can remember I've loved being around food. Chopping and frying onions until they were golden brown captivated me as a child, creating the most wonderful sounds and aromas. An onion was just something which I would cut up, cook and eat. I still love that such a simple and natural process can be so absorbing.

I was lucky to be brought up on good home-made food, but was always the first to suggest alternative ingredients to my ever patient Mum, such as bright red and green peppers instead of carrot and turnip in the family stew. Dipping my fingers in the roasting tray to sample those rich juices was a favourite activity. Like the love my own daughters, Clara and Amy, now have for running their fingers round the baking bowl and smearing the delicious flavours into their mouths.

During my school years however, cookery classes were not on the menu and I was drawn to woodwork and metalwork instead, subjects that also involved the satisfying physical process of cutting things up and creating something new. I had set my heart on being a carpenter but when my Careers teacher heard I was passionate about cooking, he persuaded me to try for that instead. That's when my resolve to become a professional chef really took hold. I left school at fifteen and was soon happy to be earning my own money as an apprentice in the kitchens of top chefs such as Michel Roux, Marco Pierre White, John Burton-Race and Nick Nairn.

I wouldn't be where I am today without the formative experience that was Le Gavroche, the London restaurant founded in the 1960s by Albert Roux. Many of the best chefs in the world have an affiliation to the Roux brothers and it was to the kitchen of Albert's son Michel Roux, that I reported in 1992 after calling to ask if I could start earlier than planned. This incredible kitchen offered the biggest challenge of my career - a highly professional, disciplined environment that really set my own standards. I can't pretend it was all fun. The place was filled with highly passionate, driven people, but the atmosphere was electric and I got to handle some of the most beautiful ingredients I'd ever seen. It was amazing to see the freshest produce from black truffles to the most unsullied vegetables coming through the doors. And it was here that I soaked in every detail about the classical preparation of food, how to work quickly and cleanly and how to organise myself.

The long hours and sheer hard work prompted many young chefs to abandon the job. But already I knew I wanted to open my own restaurant, and had started saving hard to achieve that dream.

I also loved to cook for friends and soon found myself with invitations to cook for their friends too. The social aspect of food, the way it brings people together in a kitchen or around a table has always given me a great buzz. Often something as simple as showing people how to truss up a chicken, becomes a piece of theatre which they really enjoy. And when you sit down to eat together there's immediately

the place was filled with highly passionate, driven people, but the atmosphere was electric

a common bond. It's such a pleasurable part of life.

Inspiration for my Cook School in Leith stemmed from these magical evenings. I want people to take what they learn in my school on to hosting their own dinner parties, and to give them the confidence to create this enjoyment around their own tables.

Bruce Rennie, principal tutor and Rikki Preston, pastry chef at the restaurant since 2001, join me at the Cook School in revealing many of the tips and techniques used in my kitchen. Anyone can chop an onion but there's a knack to doing it quickly and concisely with a very sharp knife. And not everyone knows how to make the most delicate pastry, peel a walnut to release its rich, full flavour, or skin and remove the guts of a pheasant.

it was a complete adrenaline rush all the way through

Nevertheless the emphasis at the Cook School isn't on the relentless routines of Michelin-starred chefs. Instead I want to encourage students to think about the flavour of ingredients and to learn the art and science of making each component taste as amazing as possible. There's lots of hands-on action. I want students to get to grips with ingredients, to be unafraid to taste throughout the preparation and cooking process. A cook needn't wait until the plate is served in the dining room before sampling flavour and texture; I want to know how a piece of sole tastes raw before I start preparing it.

I want people to taste the difference between a cold raw tomato and a tomato that's had a little salt and lemon juice added; then anchovies and fresh croutons; then salad dressed in coddled egg vinaigrette. How, I want people to ask, do each of these components taste individually and how do they taste combined? Are these flavours complementary and balanced in the final dish? That's how a professional chef thinks, and learning to do so will allow anyone to improve their cooking.

Like a painter or sculptor, it's crucial to hold what you're trying to create in the mind's eye, to imagine the finished plate and how the ingredients will come together. But what's more important is to be free from the worry of how good the end result will taste, and concentrate on the careful process of getting there. Taste constantly and make adjustments; it could lead to the discovery of a completely new flavour and teach you how to cook in an instinctive, natural way. Learning to improvise like this takes time but comes with practice.

Now, a word of warning - the recipes in this book don't hold back on ingredients the health conscious might try to reduce, such as salt, butter and sugar. But these are recipes for special occasions, not every day, and chefs all over the world will vouch for these ingredients being the key to making food feel and taste beautiful.

Back to 1999. From the first moment of turning the keys in my restaurant door to opening night was only six weeks and the priority was on making everything as clean and presentable as possible. With the support of my whole family, my Mum, my Dad and my brothers we worked from early morning until late at night to really scrub down every inch of the kitchen and give the whole place a fresh lick of paint. It didn't feel like a chore. It was a pleasure. For me it was a complete adrenaline rush all the way through.

I was so excited about the opportunity to use all that I had learned to create food in my own style and along with my wife Cecile, to serve our customers in a friendly, relaxed and comfortable way. There was also the thrill of having achieved the beginnings of my own business and becoming my own boss.

So it's ironic that this Cook Book is a set of prescriptions, with the recipes telling readers exactly what to do. But my hope is that this will only be the beginning, a means of encouraging people to find their own unique styles. To know the exhilaration of setting off on your own, independent journey is a very rich adventure.

Bring on the scene-setters, wee tantalising clues as to what will follow. Usually enjoyed informally with pre-dinner drinks, canapés should be small and uncomplicated to eat, and will ideally include enough variety to satisfy carnivores, fish lovers and vegetarians alike. Serve canapés fresh, at just the right temperature, which means planning ahead. Have ready a platter that's large enough to hold your canapés without cramming them together, and as guests get stuck in, you'll buy more precious time in the kitchen.

Canapés

HAGGIS BONBONS

1 good quality haggis approximately 400-500g
2 eggs, beaten with a little milk (egg wash)
50g plain flour
100g Panko Japanese breadcrumbs or plain breadcrumbs

Remove the haggis from its bag, and divide into small pieces weighing approximately 20g each, then roll into balls.
Lay out three bowls; one with flour, one with the egg wash and one with the breadcrumbs.
Coat the haggis balls in flour, dip into the egg to coat, then finally roll in the breadcrumbs.
Store in the fridge before cooking.
Deep fry in vegetable oil 180°C for 3 minutes then drain on kitchen paper before serving.

SMOKED HADDOCK CROQUETTES WITH PEA PURÉE

PEA PURÉE:

200g frozen peas

150ml chicken stock - *see basic 3*

50g butter

Bring the chicken stock to the boil, then add the peas and cook for 3 minutes.

Pour the peas and stock into a liquidiser and blend for 2 minutes.

Then add the butter and a little salt and blend for a further minute.

Before serving, add a few drops of white wine vinegar and mix in (this is optional).

SMOKED HADDOCK CROQUETTES:

200g undyed smoked haddock

500ml milk

1 shallot, peeled and sliced

1 sprig thyme

75g plain flour

50g unsalted butter

35g parmesan, finely grated

2 egg yolks

Beaten egg and milk (eggwash)

Panko Japanese breadcrumbs

Poach the haddock in the milk with the shallot and thyme until just cooked.

Break the fish into small flakes, pass the milk through a sieve and measure out 300ml.

Make a roux with the flour and butter, then whisk in the milk a little at a time until smooth.

Next, add the parmesan and egg yolks and whisk again until smooth.

Then add the flaked haddock.

Using a piping bag and nozzle pipe long croquettes onto a floured tray and freeze.

Cut the frozen croquettes into 2cm lengths.

Coat in a light egg and milk mixture then roll in breadcrumbs.

Store in the freezer until ready to cook.

TO SERVE:

Pre-heat a fryer to 180°C

Warm the pea purée and place a little in the centre of a ceramic spoon.

Remove the haddock croquettes from the freezer and deep fry until golden.

Season with a little salt and place on the pea purée and serve while warm.

SWEET PEPPER TARTLETS

2 firm red peppers
2 firm yellow peppers
6 tablespoons olive oil
1 clove garlic
2 sprigs fresh thyme
1 small pinch smoked sweet paprika
Bought tartlet cases approximately
45mm diameter

Cut the peppers in half lengthways.
Remove the stalk and seeds, place in a metal or glass dish and pour over the olive oil.
Slice the clove of garlic into 5, add to the peppers along with the thyme, and season with a little sea salt.
Cover with tin foil and cook in an oven 180°C (Gas mark 4) for 15 minutes, or until the peppers become soft and sweet.
When the peppers have cooled, discard the thyme and keep the juices that have collected in the cooking dish.
Peel the skin from the peppers and roughly chop them up.
Transfer into a pan with their juices and add the sweet smoked paprika.
Cook until the juices have thickened, check for seasoning and remove from the heat to cool.
Serve in small individual tartlet cases.

CHILLED SWEETCORN SOUP WITH SALTED ALMONDS

400g fresh sweetcorn
(or tinned if no fresh available)
40g unsalted butter
1 pinch saffron
250ml vegetable stock - *see basic 6*
250ml whipping cream
40g whole salted almonds, chopped
Olive oil
Salt

Melt the butter in a large pan, add the corn and saffron.
Cook on a low heat for 10 minutes stirring the corn so that it does not colour.
Pour in the vegetable stock, add a pinch of salt and boil gently for 15 minutes.
Add the cream and cook for a further 5 minutes.
Pour the soup into a liquidiser and blend until smooth.
Pass the soup through a fine mesh sieve and place in the fridge to chill.

TO SERVE:

Pour the soup into small bowls.
Add a chopped salted almond and a small teaspoon of olive oil to each bowl.

ORANGE, PARSLEY AND SPINACH JUICE

400ml fresh orange juice
12g flat leaf parsley
35g baby spinach

Pick, wash and thoroughly dry the parsley and spinach.
Pour the orange juice into a liquidiser, add the parsley and spinach and blend for 3 minutes.
Transfer to a jug and skim off the froth from the top.
Store in the fridge for at least an hour, to chill.
Give the juice a stir, then serve in shot glasses that have been chilled in the freezer.

MACADAMIA NUTS WITH BLACK OLIVES

100g white macadamia nuts
1 egg, beaten
30g plain flour
50g Panko Japanese breadcrumbs or traditional breadcrumbs
100g Provencal black olives, stoned and roughly chopped
2 tomatoes, de-seeded and diced
A few chopped chives

Select a dozen of the largest macadamia nuts and dust with flour.
In a bowl coat the nuts with beaten egg, then drain off any excess egg through a sieve and coat them in the breadcrumbs.
Store in the fridge until ready to be cooked.
Mix together the chopped olives, tomatoes and chives and set aside.

TO SERVE:

Pre-heat a fryer to 180˚C and cook the nuts for 2-3 minutes until golden.
Drain on a kitchen towel and season with salt.
Serve in a ceramic spoon with a little of the chopped olive mix.

Appetites whetted, guests, like runners on the blocks will be poised in anticipation. Delve into starters that are simple to prepare yet deliver a 'wow' factor that will get your meal off to a flying start. When choosing a starter, balance the flavour and weight of the dish carefully with other courses. And if the main dish involves lots of last-minute preparation, opt for a starter that can be made in advance, a fuss-free prelude to the main event that maintains calm in the kitchen.

Starters

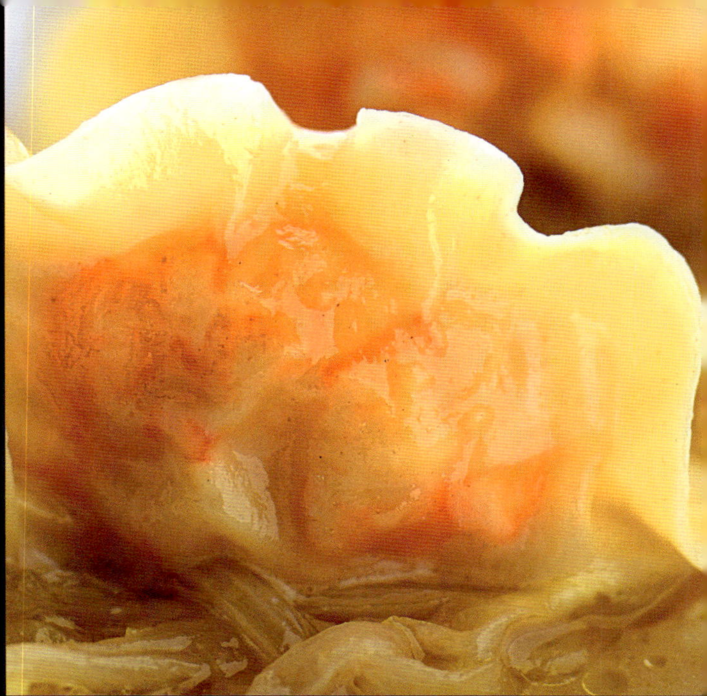

CRAB SOUP

Although velvet crabs are available all year round, they are at their best during the spring and summer seasons, and I hope this recipe will inspire you to try cooking with these and other varieties of shellfish. Velvet crabs are a lot smaller than their common brown crab cousins and with a reddish brown colour and fine coating of velvet-textured hair their name describes them perfectly. They are found on the rocky bottoms of the shoreline out to a depth of about 65m, contain less meat than the common crab, but are still packed with flavour and make a great tasting soup. This soup will keep refrigerated for up to three days or can be frozen. All the best fishmongers will be able to get hold of them for you, but they must be alive when bought, as this is nature's guarantee of freshness. Serve with good, crusty bread.

SERVES 6

CRAB SOUP

3kg velvet crabs, live and washed
150ml olive oil
125g unsalted butter
1 onion, peeled and diced
3 carrots, peeled, halved lengthways and sliced
3 sticks celery, diced
4 star anise
1 teaspoon fennel seeds
1 tablespoon mild curry powder
3 bulbs garlic, halved
6 tomatoes, halved
3 litres fish stock - *see basic 2*
½ potato, very finely sliced
½ bottle white wine
120ml double cream

Quickly sauté the crabs in a heavy-based pan with the olive oil and transfer into a colander to drain off the excess oil.
Add 75g butter to the pan, not allowing it to burn, and cook the onion, carrot and celery on a medium heat until golden brown.
Add the spices and curry powder and cook out for two minutes.
Add the white wine and reduce by half.
Add the crabs back to the pan and crush with a rolling pin.
Add the garlic and tomatoes and fish stock to cover.
Bring to the boil and cook rapidly for 30-40 minutes.
Allow to stand for a further 30 minutes off the heat before straining.
Return the strained stock to the heat with the potato and cook until the potato is soft.
Blend in a food processor with the remaining butter until smooth.
Strain through a fine sieve and adjust the seasoning.

TO SERVE:

Re-heat the soup and add 1 tablespoon of semi-whipped cream, some fresh chopped parsley and garlic croutons to each bowl.

nutty and smoky

JERUSALEM ARTICHOKE SOUP

An ingredient available in the winter, the Jerusalem artichoke is actually the root of a plant related to the sunflower. Its name is a derivation of the Italian word for sunflower - *'girasole'*. The tuber of the root looks a bit like a knobbly potato with either a pink or light brown tinged skin and a pearly white flesh. The soup needs to be prepared quickly or the artichoke will discolour. You can of course place them in water after peeling them with a drop of lemon juice and this will help to slow down any discolouration. To enable the soup to retain a light cream colour and a fresh flavour, it is important to have the stock hot before starting. The finished soup will have a slightly nutty and smoky flavour from the bacon.

SERVES 6

1kg Jerusalem artichokes
Juice ½ lemon
100g unsalted butter
1 medium onion, peeled and sliced
2 cloves garlic, peeled and sliced
100g piece lightly smoked streaky bacon
1½ litres fresh chicken stock - *see basics 3*
150ml champagne
Small handful chervil or chives, chopped
Hazelnut oil (optional)

JERUSALEM ARTICHOKE SOUP

Peel the artichokes and place them in a bowl of cold water with the juice from half a lemon to prevent them from turning brown.
Melt the butter in a large pot, add the onion and garlic and cook without colouring for 3-4 minutes.
Thinly slice the artichokes and add them to the onions.
Continue to cook for a further 5 minutes, being careful not to colour them.
Add the chicken stock and the piece of bacon, season with a couple of pinches of salt and boil the soup for 10 minutes until the artichoke becomes tender.
Remove the bacon and transfer the soup to a liquidiser.
Add the champagne and blend for 3 minutes until the soup becomes smooth and creamy. You can add a further 100g of butter if you want to make the soup richer and creamier.

TO SERVE:
Pour the soup into large bowls with some freshly chopped chervil or chives.
You could also chop the bacon into small dice and serve in the soup.
The addition of a few drops of hazelnut oil spooned on top also works very well.

CREAM OF PUMPKIN SOUP WITH SAUTÉED CEPS

Like all members of the Cucurbit family, pumpkins are an American import and our main associations with them are using them during Halloween as lanterns, although I prefer to use a turnip for this purpose! Pumpkins of course are seasonal and they keep for a long time. Serve along with Ceps - a seasonal mushroom which can be found fresh in shops that specialise in fine foods. Alternatively, you could use Ceps in a dried form or many other varieties of mushroom can be used in their place.

SERVES 6

100g unsalted butter
500g pumpkin, peeled and sliced
75g onion, peeled and sliced
500ml chicken stock, hot - *see basic 3*
10g fresh coriander (tied in muslin cloth)
200g fresh Ceps

Melt the butter in a heavy-based pot and add the sliced pumpkin and onion.
Cook this on a low heat stirring continually for around 10 minutes or until soft. Be careful not to colour the vegetables.
Add the hot chicken stock and coriander to the pan and simmer the soup for 15 minutes.
Remove the muslin bag and pour the soup into a liquidiser and blend for 10 minutes so the soup becomes silky in texture.
Wipe the Ceps clean with a damp cloth.
Slice the mushrooms and sauté them with a pinch of salt in a little butter until they are golden brown.

TO SERVE:
Serve the soup with the Ceps on top and some warm crusty bread to accompany.

LEEK AND POTATO SOUP WITH SMOKED HADDOCK

250g leeks
1 small onion
400g Finnan haddock
250ml milk (for poaching the haddock)
250ml chicken stock - *see basic 3*
150ml double cream
50g unsalted butter
1 small Yukon Gold potato
Small handful chives, chopped

Wash the leeks and discard any dark green parts.

Finely slice the onion and leeks and put to one side.

Poach the smoked haddock in the milk for 4-5 minutes and remove.

Strain the milk into a large saucepan with the stock and cream and bring it to the boil.

Melt the butter in a separate heavy-based saucepan and add the leeks and onions and cook them gently for 5-10 minutes without colouring.

Add the boiling liquid to the leeks and cook for a further 5 minutes.

Peel and finely slice the potato and add it to the pan.

Boil the soup for a further 10 minutes and remove from the heat.

Pour the soup into a liquidiser and blend for 5 minutes, so the soup becomes silky in texture.

TO SERVE:

Carefully flake the smoked haddock into 4 soup bowls using your fingers.
Warm the soup and pour it over the haddock.
Sprinkle with chopped chives and serve.

This is a very good example of how a very common soup can be made to taste luxurious by using a good cooking technique. If you slice all the vegetables involved very finely and have your stock and cream already boiling hot to go, then you are reducing the amount of time required to boil the vegetables and the soup. The maximum cooking time should be 20 - 25 minutes. Use as large a pan as possible to ensure you have more heat to cook with, as opposed to a little pan with vegetables on top of one another. The soup is served with creamy flakes of smoked haddock in the bottom of the soup bowl. Try to use the naturally smoked variety rather than the bright yellow dyed stuff, and choose a nice large fillet as this will give you larger flakes. This is similar to a soup that I serve in the restaurant and can also be served cold.

SERVES 4

This is a variation of a soup which I have eaten while visiting Mexico City. The broth is best prepared a day in advance allowing the flavours to develop together. Preparing and cooking the vegetables in larger pieces prevents them from being overcooked. When the broth is chilled you can then cut the vegetables into smaller pieces along with the beef. The onion itself has been puréed and is used to thicken the broth to give it more body. The avocado must be ripe; its creaminess works brilliantly with the sweetness of the slow cooked vegetables. With the addition of fresh lime juice and coriander, the balance of the flavours is brought full circle. SERVES 6

POACHED BEEF BROTH, AVOCADO AND LIME

POACHED BEEF BROTH, AVOCADO AND LIME

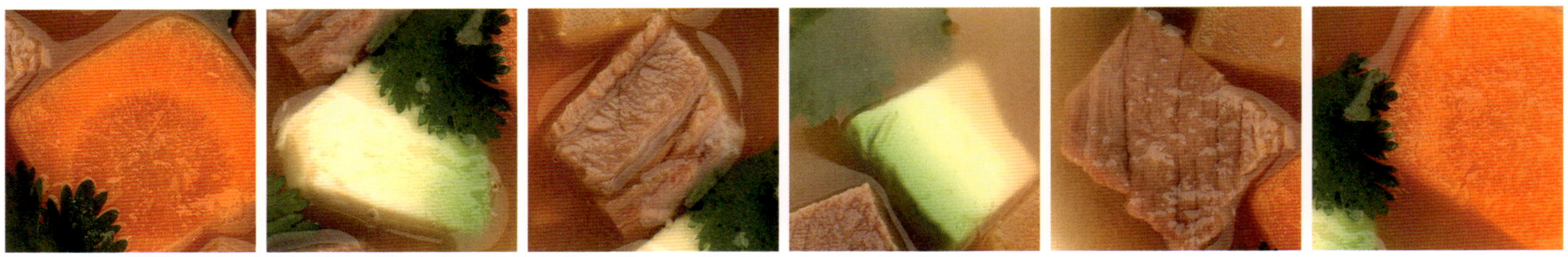

¼ yellow turnip
3 large whole carrots
½ whole onion
500g beef brisket
3 sticks celery
1 small white-skinned onion
2 ripe (Hass) avocados
1 bunch coriander
1 juicy lime
Salt

Peel the turnip, carrots and the whole onion.
Cut the carrots and onion in half lengthways.
Cut the turnip into pieces that are roughly the same size as the carrots.
Put the beef in a large pot with ½ tablespoon salt, the carrots, turnip, onion and celery and cover by 15cm of cold water.
Bring the pot to the boil, then turn the heat down to a medium simmer.
Skim off any scum that rises to the surface and cook for 2½ hours, until the beef and vegetables are tender.
Remove the soup from the heat and leave to cool.
Once cool, place the soup in the fridge for 24 hours. This will make the soup develop more flavour and is well worth doing.

THE NEXT DAY...

Remove the vegetables from the soup and discard the celery.
Cut the beef, carrots and turnip roughly into 2cm dice and put them into a pan.
Put the onion into a liquidiser with half of the stock and blend until it is smooth.
Strain this purée through a fine sieve into the pan with the vegetables.
Re-heat the soup with the vegetables and adjust the seasoning if necessary.

TO SERVE:

Chop the white onion into small dice.
Peel and cut the avocados in half, then into small dice.
Mix the onion and avocado with a little salt and put a spoonful into each bowl.
Pour the hot soup into the bowls and finish with some chopped coriander and a good squeeze of fresh lime juice.

SMOKED SALMON TARTARE WITH HORSERADISH CREAM

Smoked salmon is available all year round. It is definitely worth spending a little more on a premium grade, as taste and texture can vary dramatically. Soft oily salmon should be avoided; I prefer to use smoked organic salmon which I think has a better texture and when sliced or diced will not seep out so much oil as many traditional farmed smoked salmons often do. This recipe has a mix of caper, shallot and chives and when mixed with the salmon they work extremely well, complementing the smoky, and slightly salty, taste of the salmon. It is finished with a creamy horseradish dressing and served on top of a crisp disc of toasted brown bread. This is great to serve as a starter but also useful if you are making canapés for a dinner party.

SERVES 4

SMOKED SALMON TARTARE WITH HORSERADISH CREAM

4 thin slices brown bread cut into 6cm diameter circles
3 tablespoons olive oil + extra for toasting bread
75ml double cream
2 teaspoons horseradish sauce
200g smoked salmon
1 tablespoon capers, washed and chopped
1 small shallot, finely chopped
2 teaspoons fresh chives, finely chopped
1 tablespoon fresh chervil, finely chopped
Salt and fresh ground white pepper

Pre-heat the oven to 180˚C (Gas mark 4).
Brush each of the bread circles with a little olive oil, place on a baking tray and toast in the oven until golden brown.
Remove the toasts from the oven and set aside to cool.
Put the double cream in a bowl and whisk until soft peaks appear.
Fold the horseradish sauce into the cream and season with salt and pepper.
Store in the fridge until required.
Cut the smoked salmon into small dice with a large chopping knife.
Add the chopped capers, shallot, chives, chervil and three tablespoons of olive oil to the salmon and mix well together.
Season to taste with salt and pepper.

TO SERVE:

Place a disc of toasted brown bread in the centre of each plate and top with a small amount of the smoked salmon tartare.
Spoon some of the horseradish cream over the tartare and season with a little freshly ground pepper, serve immediately.

CARAMELISED ONION, POTATO AND GRUYÈRE TART

A delicious vegetarian dish that's similar to a quiche, where the eggs are used to set the filling. The success of this dish relies on the onions being sliced finely and evenly, then cooking them slowly so that their natural sugars are released and caramelise until the onions are golden brown. You can actually smell a noticeable difference when they have sweetened in this way, and they taste fantastic! Serve this tart warm with a leafy green salad and some good olives.

SERVES 6

100g unsalted butter
4 large onions
15 baby potatoes
400ml double cream
3 tablespoons freshly grated parmesan
4 whole eggs
100g Gruyère cheese
Salt and pepper
1 25-30cm cooked shortcrust pastry tart case

CARAMELISED ONION, POTATO AND GRUYÈRE TART

Peel the onions and slice them thinly.
Melt half of the butter in a wide pan on a gentle heat and add the onions with a pinch of salt.
Cook the onions on a medium heat, while stirring, until golden brown and sweet.
Transfer the onions to a bowl.
Cook the potatoes, skin on, in boiling salted water until just cooked.
Remove the potatoes from the water and allow them to cool completely.
Slice the potatoes in half lengthways and fry in a little oil, cut side down, until golden brown.
Remove from the pan onto paper towel to absorb the oil.
Mix the onions and potatoes and spread them evenly into the cooked pastry case.
The potatoes should stick out beyond the top of the case slightly at different angles.
Put the cream into a pan and bring it to the boil.
Add the parmesan to the cream and whisk to melt.
Turn down the heat to low and whisk the eggs into the cream and adjust the seasoning.
Stir continuously over a low heat until starting to thicken and pour over the tart mix until just below the level of the pastry.
Grate the Gruyère and sprinkle evenly over the top of the tart.
Bake in the oven at 180°C (Gas mark 4) for 10-15 minutes until the centre is just cooked.
Remove from the oven and allow the tart to stand for 10 minutes before cutting and serving.

earthy

A lot of mushrooms we buy in the local stores or supermarkets are simple button mushrooms and most of them are, of course, cultivated. The mushrooms you need for this recipe can be found in good delicatessens or specialist suppliers. Chanterelles grow in large groups, and are very tasty fried in a little butter and simply seasoned with some salt to exploit their unique earthy flavour. Ceps (*Boletus edulis*) are arguably one of the best mushrooms to eat and can be bought either fresh or dried.

SERVES 4

WILD MUSHROOM RAVIOLI WITH FRENCH BEANS AND MUSHROOM JUS

RAVIOLI FILLING AND SAUCE:

250g mixed mushrooms (Oyster, Chanterelles, Ceps, St George)
1 clove garlic
1 stem tarragon
1 shallot, finely chopped
1 egg yolk
100ml double cream
Salt and freshly ground white pepper

Clean the mushrooms, trim off any woody, dry ends of the stems and discard.
Put 50g of the cleaned mushrooms in a small saucepan along with the clove of garlic and fresh tarragon and cover with 120ml of water.
Add a small pinch of salt and boil until reduced by two thirds.
Leave to infuse for 30 minutes off the heat.
This is the mushroom stock.

Chop the remaining mushrooms into small even-sized pieces.
Sauté in a large pan with a little butter and the chopped shallot.
Season with salt and fresly ground white pepper
When they are soft, add the double cream and continue to cook until the cream has thickened and binds together with the mushrooms.
Set the mushrooms aside to cool and then mix in the egg yolk.

1 quantity fresh pasta - *see basic 13*

PREPARING RAVIOLI:

Roll out 12 discs of pasta 8cm in diameter and as thin as possible.
Place a large teaspoonful of mushrooms in the centre of each one and brush the outside with a little egg wash.
Fold over the edge to create an airtight seal.
Place each ravioli on a piece of greaseproof paper and store in the fridge until ready to cook.

FINAL PREPARATION AND SERVING:

150g extra fine French beans, cooked in salted boiling water
2 tablespoons double cream
30g cold unsalted butter, diced
3 tablespoons olive oil
½ teaspoon sherry vinegar
Salt and freshly ground white pepper

Bring a large pan of salted water to the boil.
Re-heat the mushroom stock in a pan with 2 tablespoons of double cream.
Slowly whisk in small pieces of the cold diced butter until it has emulsified.
Strain the sauce through a fine sieve and keep warm.
Split the French beans in two by separating them down the centre using your finger.
Gently warm the beans in the olive oil, add a few drops of sherry vinegar and season with salt and freshly ground pepper.
Drop the ravioli, with the paper still attached, into the boiling water and cook for 2 minutes.
Meanwhile arrange the French beans in the centre of 4 plates.
Place the cooked ravioli on top and spoon over a little mushroom jus.
Serve with a salad of mixed leaves and some soft herbs.

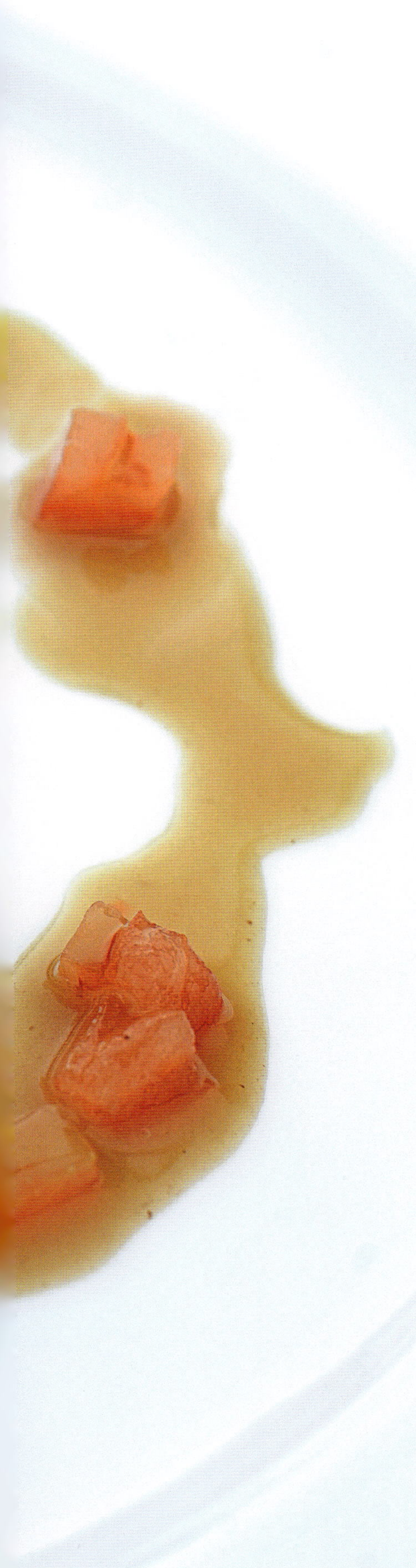

Tortellini of venison has been a very popular lunch dish in the restaurant for many years now. It is very different in flavour and texture to a piece of roasted venison loin due to the fact that it has been marinated overnight in red wine with thyme and garlic and blended to a purée, then chilled before mixing in the rich double cream and finished with a delicious port reduction. The cauliflower cream is a very good accompaniment to the tortellini as preparing it this way will intensify its flavour. You can of course serve it with many other ingredients, particularly fish - roast salmon and pan-fried scallops are two very good examples. SERVES 4

TORTELLINI OF VENISON WITH CAULIFLOWER CREAM

VENISON MOUSSE:

250g venison loin, fully trimmed of sinew and diced
120ml red wine (Cabernet Sauvignon)
1 sprig thyme
1 clove garlic, peeled and cut into 3
2 egg whites
75ml ruby port
200ml double cream
Salt and ground white pepper

Marinate the venison with the red wine, thyme and garlic in a bowl for 24 hours.
Drain the venison, discard the garlic, thyme and red wine and dry the meat on some kitchen paper.
Place the venison in a food processor, and blend for 2 minutes.
Then add the egg white and blend for a further one minute until smooth.
Pour the port into a small saucepan and reduce to a sticky glaze, allow it to cool and then add it to the venison.
Transfer the puréed venison into a large bowl and place in the fridge to chill for 30 minutes.
Slowly add the cream into the venison mixing with a spatula until fully incorporated.
Season with a pinch of salt and a few turns of fresh white pepper.
Cling film the venison and store in the fridge until ready to use.

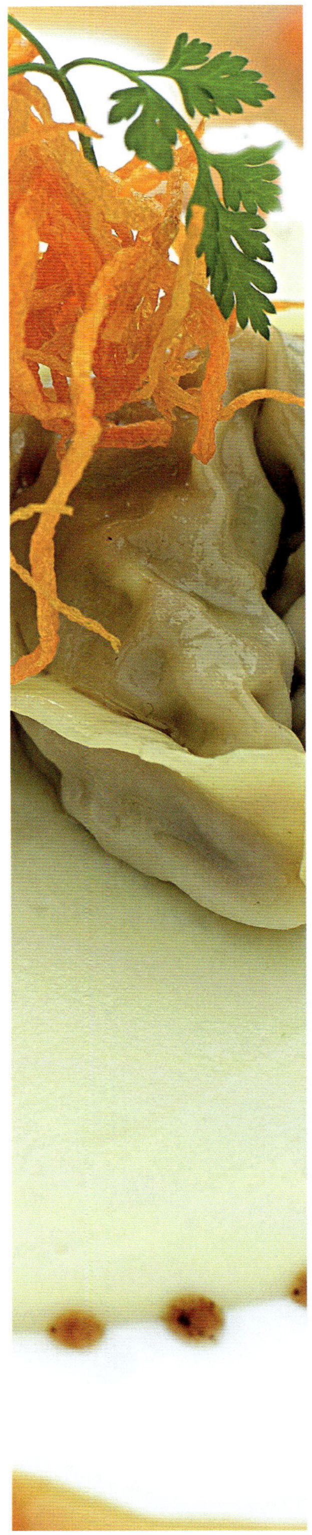

TORTELLINI:

1 quantity of pasta dough - *see basic 13*

Roll out 12 discs of pasta approximately 8cm in diameter.
Spoon a little of the venison mousse onto each one and fold over to create an airtight seal. This is ready to use as a ravioli.
Place the centre of the flat edge down on to your forefinger and bend the ravioli down around the finger.
Set the pasta down and dampen the two edges before pinching them together to seal. This is a tortellini.
Place each tortellini on a small square of greaseproof paper and refrigerate until you are ready to cook them.

CAULIFLOWER PURÉE:

1 quantity cauliflower purée - *see basic 21*

COOKING AND SERVING THE TORTELLINI:

Bring a large pan of water to the boil with a couple pinches of salt, drop in the tortellini while still attached to the paper and cook for 3 minutes.
Meanwhile re-heat the cauliflower purée, place two or three spoonfuls in the centre of each plate, gently tapping the bottom of the plate so the purée flattens out.
Arrange the tortellini around the purée and serve.

LANGOUSTINE RISOTTO WITH PARMESAN

Langoustines have a much sweeter taste than lobster and should be bought fresh and alive but these can be difficult to find so I suggest you use very fresh - or even frozen - ones from a good fishmonger. They should be boiled quickly for 1-2 minutes in heavily salted water, straight from the sea if possible, which will enhance their true seafood flavour. For this recipe you need to use a good base stock, I recommend using the heads of the langoustines, which are full of flavour. Cook the risotto slowly adding the stock ladle by ladle, stirring all the time. Garnish with freshly shaved parmesan cheese.

SERVES 4

LANGOUSTINE RISOTTO WITH PARMESAN

FOR THE RISOTTO:

50g unsalted butter
1 clove garlic, peeled and finely diced
½ onion, finely diced
150g Arborio or Carnaroli risotto rice
400-500ml langoustine stock, hot - *see basic 1*
50g freshly grated parmesan
75g mascarpone cheese
Salt and freshly ground white pepper
Cooked langoustines to serve (approx 4-6 each)

Melt the butter in a wide-based pan and gently cook the garlic and onion for 2 minutes without colouring.
Add the rice to the pan and stir well to coat the rice with butter.
Add the stock a little at a time, stirring continually so that the rice cooks evenly and does not stick, until it is almost cooked.
Next add the parmesan and mascarpone cheese and mix in well.
Adjust the seasoning with salt and white pepper and set aside.

TO SERVE:

Spoon the risotto into four large bowls, arrange cooked langoustines on top and sprinkle with some freshly shaved parmesan.
Serve with a side salad.

Note: *To ensure you have a perfectly cooked risotto with no 'bite' to the rice, keep tasting the rice towards the end of the cooking time. You may find you need a little less, or more, stock depending on the heat and size of your pan.*

luxurious lobster

Related to the crab, the luxurious lobster is by far the classier relative and cold water lobsters from northern seas are believed to be the finest. The European wild lobster, among which the royal blue lobster of Audresselles resides, is pricier than the larger American (Maine) lobster, but was greatly appreciated by the royal and aristocratic families of France and the Netherlands as depicted in Dutch paintings of the 16th and 17th centuries. Lobster is best eaten fresh and normally purchased live. Once killed, the flesh deteriorates very quickly, so the best way of ensuring freshness is to cook it straight after it's been killed or to cook it live. Lobster has a sweet tasting, sumptuous flesh which is low in fat, rich in minerals and bursting with flavour. Although lobsters can grow to be quite large, the smaller ones are tender and best eaten between 650g and 1.4kg.

Spring rolls are fried Chinese pastries which are filled with a variety of fillings including meat, shellfish and vegetables. They are usually eaten during the Spring Festival in China (hence the name) and are delicious accompanied by a dipping sauce to complement the flavours within. Salsa in Spanish means 'sauce' and is traditionally made with chopped tomatoes, onions, chillies and peppers. In this case, mango and basil salsa goes well with the sweet-flavoured flesh of the lobster and the chillies help to give it a bit of a kick.

SERVES 6

LOBSTER SPRING ROLL WITH MANGO SALSA

FOR THE LOBSTER:

2 whole lobsters, approx. 750g each
2 carrots, diced
1 onion, diced
2 sticks celery, diced
1 star anise
2 litres water
Salt

Place all the ingredients except the lobster into a pan, bring to the boil and simmer it for 4 minutes.
Kill the lobsters by piercing the centre of the head with a large knife and cutting down and through quickly and efficiently.
Add the lobsters to the simmering pan and remove it from the heat.
Allow to stand for 15 minutes and remove the lobsters from the pan with a slotted spoon.
Crack the claw and tail shells and remove the meat carefully.
Cut the lobster into 1.5cm dice, cover and set aside.

FOR THE SPRING ROLLS:

2 tablespoons peanut oil
1 tablespoon sesame oil
1 clove garlic, peeled and very finely chopped
2cm piece fresh ginger, peeled and very finely diced
6 fresh shiitake mushrooms, sliced
2 leeks, cut into 8cm lengths and finely shredded
Salt and pepper
6 spring roll wrappers
6 leaves Savoy cabbage, finely shredded with the centre stalk removed
6 spring onions, sliced finely on the diagonal
100g white radish, cut the same as the leeks
A little paste made with flour and cold water

Gently fry the garlic and ginger in the peanut and sesame oils for 2 minutes without colouring.
Add the mushrooms and leeks and cook for a further 5 minutes until the leeks are soft.
Season to taste with salt and pepper and set aside.
Lay the spring roll wrappers with one corner nearest you to form a diamond.
Start filling two thirds from the front.
Place an even amount of cabbage on each wrapper in a horizontal line.
Below this place a line of mushroom and leek mix, then the lobster.
Finish with a thin line of the white radish and spring onion.
Brush the edges of the wrapper with a small amount of the flour paste.
Fold the top corner of the wrapper towards you and roll into a cylinder, tucking the sides in as you go.
When required, shallow fry the spring rolls in vegetable oil for about 40 seconds on each side until golden brown and crisp.

FOR THE SALSA:

1 large mango, cut into 1cm dice, trimmings set aside
½ medium red chilli, seeds removed and diced very finely
1 teaspoon fresh ginger, peeled and very finely sliced
1 teaspoon peanut oil
1 tablespoon caster sugar
1 tablespoon rice vinegar
8 large leaves basil, sliced very finely with a sharp knife

Gently fry the chilli and ginger in the oil for 2 minutes without colouring.
Add the sugar, vinegar and mango trimmings to the pan and cook on a medium heat until the fruit breaks down.
Remove from the heat.
Stir in the diced mango flesh and allow to chill in the fridge until needed.
Stir in the basil 10 minutes before serving.

Guinea fowl is the rather under-appreciated cousin of the chicken. The meat is a tanned brown in colour with a subtle flavour, less gamey than pheasant or grouse. Generally a whole guinea fowl will serve two people. If you prefer you can substitute the guinea fowl with chicken, or even salmon, and use the same method for cooking the dish as the same principles apply.

It's important when preparing this dish that the ingredients are chilled, and to use a good food processor to ensure that you achieve the smooth consistency for the sausage. I know it might look like there has been quite a lot of cream used in this dish but the amount of cream in this recipe is in direct relation to the amount of meat. Double cream is also the best cream to use for its smooth consistency.

SERVES 6

BOUDIN OF GUINEA FOWL WITH LEEK CREAM

GUINEA FOWL BOUDIN:

200g guinea fowl breast meat
1 egg white
250ml double cream
1 tablespoon brandy
Salt

Place the meat in a food processor and blend until smooth.
Add the egg white and brandy and blend until well mixed.
Transfer the contents from the blender into a large metal bowl, cling film and place in the fridge to chill for twenty minutes.
With a plastic spatula, slowly add the cream, stirring continuously, until it is fully incorporated.
Season with a pinch of salt and transfer the mousse into a piping bag with a plain nozzle.
On a work surface lay out a 30cm square piece of cling film and pipe out a 10cm long 'boudin' (sausage).
Roll over the cling film and fold in the sides to form a firm cylinder.
Repeat until all the mousse is finished.
You should have enough to make about 8 to 10 boudins.
Cook in a steamer for 10 minutes.
Leave the boudins in the cling film until ready to serve.

1 quantity leek cream - *see basic 16*

TO SERVE:

Unwrap the warm guinea fowl boudins and cut each one into three even-sized slices.
Gently sauté the boudins in a little olive oil using a non-stick pan until golden brown. Be careful as they colour very quickly.
Spoon some of the leek cream onto the centre of each plate, arrange the sliced boudins around the leek and serve immediately.

1.4kg farmed, not wild, rabbit legs
3 tablespoons olive oil
150g smoked bacon, diced
1 carrot, peeled and diced
1 small onion, peeled and diced
500ml Chablis white wine
2 pig's trotters
1½ litres chicken stock - *see basics 3*
Tied in a piece of muslin to form a bag:
 10 white peppercorns
 10 black peppercorns
 2 bay leaves
 1 small bunch of thyme
2 tablespoons grain mustard
3 tablespoons parsley, chopped
1 tablespoon tarragon, chopped
Salt and freshly ground pepper
28cm terrine mould or 12 individual ramekins
Pre-heat the oven to 140°C (Gas mark 1)

Heat the olive oil in a large pan, sauté the rabbit legs on all sides until golden brown.

Add the diced onion, carrot and bacon and sauté until golden brown.

Pour in the white wine and cook for one minute, add the pig's trotters, the muslin bag of peppercorns and herbs, and pour over the chicken stock. Bring to a simmer.

Add a pinch of salt, cover with a lid and place in the oven to braise for 1½ hours.

Remove from the oven and leave to cool to body temperature.

Pick all the meat off the bones and shred finely between your fingers in a large bowl.

Pass the cooking stock through a fine sieve into a pan, return the carrot and onion to the meat.

Boil the cooking stock and reduce by one third, skimming to remove any fat and scum.

Then pour back over the shredded rabbit.

Mix in the mustard and chopped herbs and check the seasoning, adding salt and pepper as needed.

Transfer into a terrine mould or individual ramekins, refrigerate for at least 12 hours.

Serve with some toasted bread and mixed salad dressed with tarragon vinegar and a good olive oil.

BRAISED POTTED RABBIT LEGS

Rabbit is often regarded as a difficult meat to cook with, although this is actually far from the truth. Slim tenderloins taken from the back of a rabbit can be slowly roasted until slightly pink, whilst the legs can be used in a casserole or slowly confited in duck fat - tastes fantastic! It provides a lean and healthy meal with a flavour and texture similar to organic or free-range chicken.

For this particular recipe, a couple of pig's trotters should be cooked along with the rabbit legs, providing a gelatinous stock. Best results are obtained when the rabbit legs are cooked and left to soak in the stock. The meat can then be broken up between the fingers whilst the remaining stock is reduced by boiling. This further intensifies the flavour before it gets added back to the rabbit meat. Mix in a good spot of mustard and leave to set firm in the fridge. Serve with some toasted bread and a good glass of Chablis wine.

SERVES 12-16

RILLETTES OF DUCK AND PORK

200g skinless pork back fat
350g tinned duck fat (for confit)
250ml cold water
600g duck leg meat, skin and bones removed
(approximately 1-2kg whole legs.)
400g pork shoulder, diced
1 small whole onion, peeled
2 whole carrots, peeled
3 cloves garlic, peeled
150ml white wine (Chablis)
1 tablespoon salt
Tied in a piece of muslin to form a bag:
- 1 small bunch fresh thyme
- 2 bay leaves
- 20 white peppercorns
- 20 black peppercorns
- 2 whole star anise
- 3 whole cloves

2 teaspoons green peppercorns
1 tablespoon parsley, chopped
28cm terrine mould or 12 individual ramekins

Cut the pork fat into 2cm cubes, place in a large pot along with the tinned duck fat, add the cold water and place on a low / medium heat to gently simmer, cooking for 30-40 minutes making sure that it does not catch on the base of the pan.

Cut the duck meat into large cubes, approximately the same size as the diced pork, then add both meats to the pot with the whole onion, carrots, garlic, white wine, salt and the muslin bag of herbs and spices.

Cook this over a low heat so it is gently simmering for 2½ to 3 hours, so that the meat is very tender and you can crumble it easily between your fingers.

When cooked, remove the pan from the stove and leave to cool down to body temperature.

Remove and discard the muslin bag and the whole onion. Using your hands, gently break down the meat and the carrots until everything has been finely shredded and the fat has been mixed in well.

Check the seasoning and adjust if required, using salt and freshly ground pepper.

Mix in the whole green pepper corns and chopped parsley.

Transfer into clean terrine or paté moulds and refrigerate for at least 12 hours.

Serve with toasted brown bread and a salad of rocket and watercress dressed with red wine vinegar and good olive oil.

This is a great rustic and classical French regional dish. It is very easy to make but takes a while to cook. Serve it with toasted brown bread and a salad of rocket and watercress dressed with red wine vinegar and good olive oil.

SERVES 12-16

LANGOUSTINE AND ROCKET

I find rocket to be one of the most interesting salads to work with. Its peppery taste can be intense on its own; therefore it is better mixed with other ingredients. Within this recipe the rocket is actually wilted into the pasta at the last minute and served with roasted langoustine tails and shavings of parmesan.

SERVES 4

1 quantity fresh pasta - *see basic 13*

ROLLING & COOKING THE PASTA:

Roll out the pasta as thin as you can (using a pasta machine) then cut into thin even strips using a sharp knife.
Place the pasta into salted water; it will only take 30 seconds to cook.
Cool down under cold running water, then drain off and mix with a little olive oil and place aside until you are ready to re-heat and serve.

TO SERVE:

1 quantity langoustine cappuccino sauce - *see basic 7*
50g rocket leaves
100g good quality Parmigiano Reggiano
16 langoustine tails, cooked and peeled

Gently warm the langoustine sauce in a pan.
Drop the pasta into boiling water to reheat.
Then strain through a sieve.
Add one third of the langoustine sauce to the warm pasta followed by the rocket.
Arrange in four large bowls. Shave the parmesan over the top.
Pan-fry the langoustine tails in a little olive oil and arrange on the pasta.
Whizz the remaining sauce with a hand blender to create a cappuccino effect.
Spoon over each dish and serve immediately.

Mussels are best to eat during the colder months of the year. I particularly like the ones farmed in Walls, Shetland by a company called Demlane. It's also where my Dad is from and is a very beautiful part of the Shetland Isles. The mussels are grown in cold, clear deep water which makes them plump with a creamy orange colour.

When buying your mussels make sure the shells are closed or if they are very fresh that they close themselves when handled. This dish can be served as a starter or alternatively as a canapé at a dinner party. The shallot cream, which is served in the mussel shell with the mussel on top, is also delicious with roast sea bass or halibut. A mixture of ground almonds and fresh parmesan is used to coat the top of the mussels before being browned under the grill which will fill your kitchen with a mouth-watering aroma.

SERVES 6

MUSSELS SERVED IN THE SHELL WITH SHALLOT CREAM AND ALMOND GRATIN

PREPARING AND COOKING THE MUSSELS:

2kg mussels, washed, cleaned and de-bearded
50g unsalted butter
3 sticks celery
2 carrots, peeled
2 cloves garlic, sliced
200ml white wine (Sauvignon Blanc)

Chop the carrot and celery into 1cm dice.
Melt the butter in a pan large enough to take all the mussels. Otherwise cook them in two batches.
Put the carrot, celery and garlic into the pan and cook over a low heat for 2-3 minutes.
Pour in the white wine, turn up the heat to full, then add all the mussels and cover with a tight-fitting lid.
After 3-4 minutes turn the mussels over with a large spoon and cover again with the lid.
Cook for a further 5 minutes or until the shells are completely open.
Remove from the heat and strain through a large colander, saving the juices.
Pick out and discard the vegetables.
Remove the mussels from their shells, saving enough of the largest shells to serve the mussels in.
Store the mussels in the fridge until ready to serve.

1 quantity shallot cream - *see basic 17*
stored in the fridge until ready to serve

ALMOND GRATIN:

200g ground almonds
50g fresh parmesan, finely grated
1 tablespoon parsley, chopped

Mix all of the ingredients together in a bowl.

TO FINISH AND SERVE:

Arrange the mussel shells on a metal tray.
Spoon a small amount of shallot cream into each shell.
Place a mussel on top, then sprinkle over a good coating of the almond and parmesan mixture.
Cook under a hot grill or in the oven 200°C (Gas mark 6) until the tops are a crisp golden brown.
Serve immediately on a large platter.

CRISPY OYSTER BEIGNETS

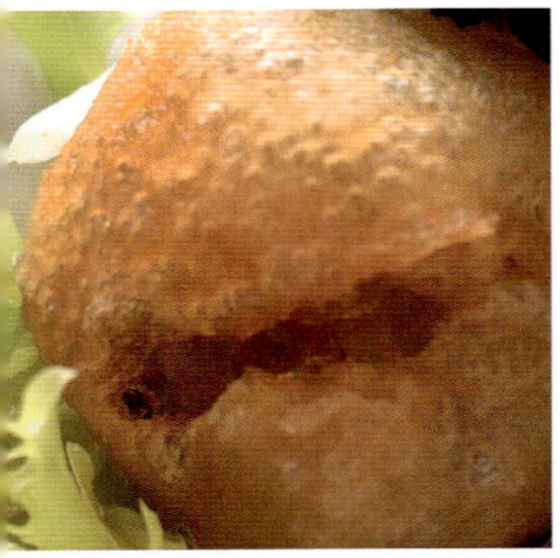

Here is a dish in which the textures play an important part. The crisp beignet, which is basically a fresh yeast batter, coats the outside of the creamy oyster. Serve hot with some freshly chopped chive and ginger which has been mixed with groundnut oil. It is a great alternative to eating raw oysters. Ensure that the oysters are tightly closed when you buy them. When you are ready to open them place a folded dish cloth in the palm of your hand as this will allow you to get a good grip on the oyster and will protect your hand should the oyster knife slip. Hold the rounded part of the shell with the flat side uppermost and place the knife in the hinge of the shell. Applying a steady pressure, move the knife up and down scraping along the underside of the shell to release the oyster. Use a teaspoon to scoop out the oyster, remembering to keep the rounded half of the shell to serve them in. This may seem like a difficult task, but with a few attempts you will succeed - just buy a few extra!

SERVES 6

24 fresh rock oysters
160ml beer
15g fresh yeast (or 7g dried yeast)
110g plain flour, plus extra for flouring oysters
5 tablespoons peanut oil (groundnut)
30g fresh root ginger
Salt
50g chives
Juice ½ lemon
1 tablespoon light soy sauce
Small bag continental mixed leaves (washed and dried)

Deep fat fryer or stove top fryer set to max (180°C-200°C)
Open the oysters with an oyster knife, being careful not to damage the flesh.
Rinse the oysters in their own liquid to remove any fragments of shell and place into a container, straining the liquid over them through a fine sieve.
Trim the shells to a neat and even finish with a pair of scissors and boil them in a pan for 10 minutes to sterilise.
Warm the beer to body temperature being careful not to exceed 36°C or the yeast will die.
Crumble the yeast into a bowl and gradually whisk in the beer until smooth.
Add the flour, mixing to make a smooth batter.
Dust very lightly with a little flour, cover with cling film and leave to prove at room temperature for 15-20 minutes.
Peel the ginger and slice very finely, then cut these slices into very fine dice and store in 2 tablespoons of peanut oil and a little salt to taste.
Use a very sharp knife to finely chop the chives and mix with the ginger with just enough oil to bind the mixture.
Mix the lemon juice, soy and remaining 3 tablespoons oil in a bowl and dress the salad leaves with this.
Dry the oysters on a clean towel and lightly dust with the flour.
Dip each oyster into the batter so that they are fully coated and carefully drop into the hot fryer until golden brown and crispy.
Drain on fresh kitchen towel. Lightly season each oyster with a squeeze of lemon juice and a pinch of salt.

TO SERVE:

Place a little of the dressed leaves into each shell (4 per plate).
Place one beignet onto each shell and top with a little of the chive and ginger mix.

Note: *This must be plated fairly quickly or the batter will soften.*

Tuna is the largest member of the mackerel family - the flesh is more akin to the texture of meat. It is both delicious and healthy to eat and makes a welcome change served as a late summer salad. Buy it fresh from the fishmonger, and I would recommend that you ask for line caught blue fin tuna although yellow fin makes fine eating too. Ask for a centre loin cut and avoid anything that is bruised or has blood lines through it.

GRILLED TUNA LOIN, LITTLE GEM AND CODDLED EGG VINAIGRETTE

I love the vinaigrette prepared this way, as the olive oil and creamy coddled eggs completely coat the salad leaves. When I prepare this at home with my daughters, Clara and Amy, they have great fun helping to crush the eggs with a fork and mixing in the vinaigrette together. The simple preparation of the tomatoes needs to be done in advance to help intensify their flavour. Serve the salad with some toasted bread or boiled new potatoes if you want to serve it as a main course.

SERVES 6

GRILLED TUNA LOIN, LITTLE GEM AND CODDLED EGG VINAIGRETTE

TOMATOES:

6 firm red plum tomatoes
Drizzle olive oil
Pinch salt
Pinch caster sugar
2 cloves garlic

Cut a small cross in the bottom of the tomatoes and peel them by dropping into a pan of boiling water for 30 seconds and then straight into a bowl of iced water.
Remove the skin and cut the tomatoes vertically into quarters.
Cut out and discard the seeds to leave you with the flesh.
Place the tomatoes in a bowl with a pinch each of salt and sugar and a drizzle of olive oil.
Toss gently to coat.
Arrange the tomatoes on a cooling or cake rack and top with the garlic, peeled and cut into very thin slices.
Leave the tomatoes in a warm place or an oven at 70°C until lightly dried. This will take 60-90 minutes.

CODDLED EGG VINAIGRETTE:

3 medium eggs
4 tablespoons extra virgin olive oil
3 tablespoons peanut oil / groundnut oil
1 tablespoon white wine vinegar
Pinch salt

Cook the eggs in a pan of boiling water for 4 minutes and then leave under a running cold tap until cool.
Whisk together the oils, vinegar and salt until well combined.
Peel the eggs into a bowl and break down with a fork.
Stir with the fork and drizzle in the vinaigrette to mix well.
The egg whites should give texture to the dressing and the soft yolks a creaminess.

TO FINISH AND SERVE:

6 x 100g fresh tuna loin steaks
3 heads Little Gem lettuce

Break the lettuce down into individual leaves, place in a bowl with the tomatoes and dress with the vinaigrette.
Divide the salad between six plates.
Season the tuna with salt, place it onto a metal tray and drizzle with olive oil.
Cook the tuna under a pre-heated hot grill for 2 minutes or until it is cooked, but still pink in the centre.
Season with a twist of freshly ground pepper and place on top of the salad.

a pleasure to make as they are to eat

LANGOUSTINE RAVIOLI, BRAISED ORANGE ENDIVE AND LANGOUSTINE CAPPUCCINO SAUCE

These langoustine ravioli, which are wrapped in a thin, almost transparent, jacket of freshly rolled pasta and served with a simple and quick endive garnish, are as much of a pleasure to make as they are to eat.

SERVES 6

LANGOUSTINE RAVIOLI, BRAISED ORANGE ENDIVE AND LANGOUSTINE CAPPUCCINO SAUCE

BRAISED ENDIVE:

300g endive, finely sliced
60g unsalted butter
35g caster sugar
1 tablespoon sherry vinegar
The juice of 1 orange

Melt the butter in a pan; add the endive and sauté for 2-3 minutes.
Add the sugar, and as it starts to caramelise, add the sherry vinegar, then the orange juice.
Cook for a further 1 minute or until the liquid has reduced by two thirds remove the pan from the heat and set aside.

RAVIOLI:

1.5kg langoustines
200g pasta dough - *see basic 13*

Separate the tails from the langoustine heads (keep the heads for the stock); remove the intestinal tract from the tails by gently pulling away the central tail fin.
Drop the tails into a pan of heavily salted water for 10 seconds, then remove immediately onto a tray to cool.
Peel away the shells, and then chop the tails to form a coarse filling.
Roll out a fine sheet of pasta and cut out 12 discs 8-10cm wide.
Place a spoonful of chopped langoustine in the centre, brush the edge of the pasta with a little water and fold over to form an airtight parcel.
Place each ravioli on a small square of greaseproof paper and refrigerate until you are ready to cook them.

TO SERVE:

1 quantity langoustine cappuccino sauce - *see basic 7*

Bring a large pan of salted water to the boil and carefully drop the ravioli, still on the greaseproof paper, into the pan and cook for 90 seconds.
Serve with the braised endive and the langoustine sauce.

BOUDIN OF SCALLOP
WITH LEMON GRASS CAPPUCCINO

The fantastic Scottish hand dived scallops that we use at the restaurant are a delight to work with. The meat is really sweet and firm and is enclosed in tightly shut shells. The firm, but delicate, touch required to remove them from their shells is a skill all serious chefs need to have mastered!

SERVES 6

BOUDIN:

200g scallop meat
2 egg whites
Squeeze lemon juice
Small pinch cayenne pepper
80ml double cream
Pinch salt

Note: *Ensure all ingredients have been chilled for at least 1 hour.*

In a food processor, blend the scallops for 1 minute, then add the egg whites, lemon juice and cayenne and blend for a full 30 seconds until completely smooth.
Transfer the contents of the blender into a large metal bowl, cling film and place in the fridge to chill for twenty minutes.
With a plastic spatula, slowly add the cream, stirring continuously, until fully incorporated. Season with a pinch of salt and transfer into a piping bag with a plain nozzle.
On a work surface lay out a 30cm square piece of cling film and pipe out a 10cm long 'boudin' (sausage).
Roll over the cling film and fold in the sides to form a firm cylinder.
Repeat until all the mousse is finished.
You should have enough to make about 8 to 10 boudins.
Cook in a steamer for 8 minutes. Leave the boudins in the cling film until ready to serve.

TO SERVE:

1 quantity lemon grass cappuccino - *see basic 12*
125g baby spinach

Unwrap the scallop boudins and cut each one into three even-sized pieces.
Gently sauté in a little olive oil using a non-stick pan until golden brown. Be careful, the boudins colour very quickly.
Cook the spinach in a little salted water with a small knob of butter.
Arrange a plate with some cooked spinach and the boudins.
Gently warm the sauce to 75°C and use a hand blender or whisk to create a cappuccino foam, spoon around the scallop boudins before serving.

WARM SALAD OF WILD MUSHROOMS, WATERCRESS AND BALSAMIC VINEGAR

I often use mushrooms in my recipes and there is such a fantastic selection of varieties, sizes and flavours available. For this dish I have used Girolles, Hedgehog and Pied de Mouton mushrooms, which can be sourced from your local farmers' market or delicatessen. Wild mushrooms can also be picked throughout the year, if you know what you are looking for and are knowledgeable in picking the correct species. Wild mushrooms can also be cultivated and are available in supermarkets.

I buy my mushrooms throughout the year from a number of mushroom suppliers across Scotland and France. There is an abundant choice of mushroom varieties available in Scotland. Three varieties that I use regularly in the restaurant are Girolles, which have a delicious autumnal earthy taste, Ceps, which are one of my favourite mushrooms and have a meaty taste and texture, and the Black Trumpet mushroom.

SERVES 6

1kg mixed wild mushrooms e.g. Oyster, Girolles, Hedgehog, Pied de Mouton
2 slices day old white bread, crusts removed
2 cloves garlic
2 shallots
5 tablespoons olive oil
1 tablespoon balsamic vinegar
250g fresh watercress
Salt

Prepare the mushrooms by removing any tough stalks and cutting down into evenly sized strips.
Wash the prepared mushrooms quickly in a large basin of water and remove excess water by spinning them in a salad spinner, then leave to air dry on a wire rack for 30 minutes.
Peel one of the garlic cloves and cut it in half.
Add it to a pan with 2 tablespoons of the olive oil and heat it to infuse.
Cut the bread into 1cm squares and fry these in the olive oil on a medium heat until golden brown.
Drain through a colander or sieve and dry on paper towel.
Lightly season the croutons with salt and remove the garlic.
Put the remaining oil into a wide-based pan.
Peel and dice the shallots finely and fry in the oil for 30 seconds.
Add the remaining garlic, peeled and halved, to the pan and then add the mushrooms in one even layer.
Season with a little salt and sauté until golden brown. Transfer to a mixing bowl.
Add the balsamic vinegar to the mushrooms while still hot.
Remove the garlic and allow them to cool a little.

WARM SALAD OF WILD MUSHROOMS, WATERCRESS AND BALSAMIC VINEGAR

TO FINISH AND SERVE:

Remove and discard the watercress stalks and rinse the leaves in cold water.
Toss the leaves into the lukewarm mushrooms and arrange on a plate.
Top the salad with the croutons and serve.

SALAD OF FRENCH BEANS WITH HAZELNUTS

This is a delicious salad which is not only colourful, but full of goodness. French green beans are a very thin variety of green bean that are crisp and tender and are an excellent source of vitamins A and C. They also contain heart-friendly nutrients, including potassium and magnesium, which help to maintain a healthy blood pressure. Whilst they are a more expensive variety of bean, they are worth buying and taste delicious served in salads. This particular recipe is full of texture and flavour and I have used chervil, a delicate annual herb, which is usually used to season mild-flavoured foods, and young vegetables. Some cooks refer to chervil as 'gourmet's parsley' and it gives a distinctive flavour to the dish. **SERVES 4**

500g extra fine green beans
180g whole hazelnuts
4 tablespoons crème fraîche
1 teaspoon Dijon mustard
Juice ½ lemon
Sea salt and freshly ground white pepper
2 tablespoons fresh chervil, chopped
120-150g mixed salad leaves

Place a large salad serving bowl into the fridge to chill.
Bring a large pan of salted water to the boil and drop in the beans.
Prepare a large bowl of ice cold water for the beans.
After 4-5 minutes check to see if they are cooked (they should just have a little bite to them).
When cooked, drain them quickly and plunge them into the cold water.
This will stop them cooking and will help retain their colour.
Drain them quickly and dry them on a cloth.
Cut the hazelnuts into halves with a sharp knife, heat a non-stick sauté pan and toast the nuts until golden, stirring them to prevent them over-colouring. Alternatively you can toast them in the oven.
Set aside to cool.
30 minutes before you are ready to serve, remove the bowl from the fridge.
Combine the crème fraîche, lemon juice, Dijon mustard, a pinch of salt and some ground white pepper and whisk together.
Add the chopped chervil, sliced hazelnuts and French beans.
Toss together with a wooden spoon, check the seasoning and serve with some mixed leaves tossed in a little olive oil and lemon juice.

SALAD OF FRENCH BEANS
WITH HAZELNUTS

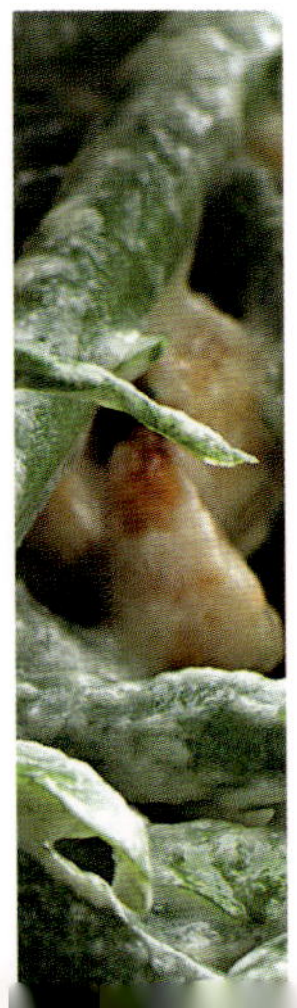

Like pottering about in a boat, a great meal with friends causes hours to disappear. Match the luxury of time with the luxurious treasures of our Scottish seas - fish and shellfish including scallops, lobster and langoustine - also in high demand from top European chefs. Whether you're up for a spot of hand diving or just know a great fishmonger, I've included diverse possibilities for the preparation of your catch, from poaching and steaming to rapid cooking and roasting.

Fish

STEAMED SALMON WRAPPED IN BACON WITH ROSEMARY BUTTER SAUCE

Salmon is very versatile and can be cooked in a wide variety of ways, from baking and grilling to smoking and frying, always guaranteeing a quick, healthy and tasty dish. Salmon and bacon complement each other well, especially if you steam the salmon and wrap it in smoked bacon. This allows the fish to absorb the smoky, meaty flavour and is superb served with a light side-dish of salad or green vegetables. SERVES 4

4 portions of organic salmon, 130g each
8 thin slices of lightly smoked bacon
1 large carrot
½ a leek
2 tablespoons white wine vinegar
3 sprigs fresh rosemary
100ml double cream
120g unsalted butter
150g fresh Girolle mushrooms or small white button mushrooms
16 new potatoes, peeled and boiled

Wrap each piece of salmon with 2 slices of bacon and brush it with a little olive oil.
Place the fish in a dish, cover with cling film and leave in the fridge for 12 hours to allow the bacon's flavour to penetrate the salmon.
Peel the carrot and wash the leek, then cut them into small even dice and cook separately in salted boiling water until tender.
Put the vinegar, rosemary and cream into a small saucepan, and simmer for a couple of minutes.
Then slowly whisk in the cold diced butter a little at a time until fully incorporated, making sure that the sauce does not boil.
When done, remove the rosemary and keep in a warm place at around room temperature.
Place a steamer on the stove and bring to the boil.
Season each portion of salmon with a little salt, then place them in the steamer to cook (allow 10-15 minutes, depending on the thickness of the salmon).
Clean the mushrooms and if they are large cut into quarters.
Then gently sauté them in a little butter until tender.
Warm the leek and carrots in the sauce, then add the cooked mushrooms.
Warm the cooked new potatoes, then add a little knob of butter and lightly crush them with a fork.

TO SERVE:
On a warm plate, place a spoonful of the crushed potato followed by a piece of salmon.
Gently spoon a little of the sauce and vegetables over the top and serve immediately.

STEAMED HALIBUT WITH CABBAGE AND ROSEMARY

Steaming fish is a healthy and versatile method of cooking as it extracts the true flavour of what you are eating. Correct seasoning with a good quality sea salt is essential and steaming with different herbs and spices will allow you to infuse different flavours with the minimum amount of preparation. This main course is a good example - it is a simple and easy dish to prepare and cook. Sweet seasonal Savoy cabbage, shown the pan before steaming, provides a nutritious and tasty accompaniment for the halibut which is steamed with the sensational flavour and aroma of the rosemary. Alternatively, you can use salmon or even haddock. Prepare the ingredients up to two hours in advance, but only steam the fish 10 minutes before serving.

SERVES 6

6 x 150g portions halibut
1 small head Savoy cabbage
2 sprigs rosemary, one left whole and the other finely chopped
1 lemon
1 teaspoon pink peppercorns, coarsely crushed
2 tablespoons extra virgin olive oil
Salt and freshly ground white pepper

Remove and discard the tougher outer leaves of the cabbage and cut it into quarters.
Remove the thick stems and break the leaves into smaller pieces.
Bring a large pan of well salted water to the boil and cook the cabbage for 6 to 8 minutes until tender.
Drain and cool the cabbage in a colander under cold running water. Drain again and set aside.
Fill a fish steamer or a large pot with water into which a bamboo steamer will fit.
Add a sprig of rosemary, juice of half the lemon and 2 pinches of salt to the water and bring to the boil with a tight-fitting lid so a good steam rises.
Place the cabbage leaves in the centre of the steamer, sprinkle with half of the chopped rosemary and half of the pink peppercorns, season with a little salt and ground white pepper.
Season each fillet of halibut with some ground sea salt, the remaining chopped rosemary and pink peppercorns.
Place the fish on top of the cabbage and steam over a high heat for 5-10 minutes, depending on the thickness of the halibut, until cooked through.

TO SERVE:
Arrange the cabbage and halibut on a large plate.
Drizzle the fish with olive oil and the juice from the remaining lemon half.
Serve immediately.

The sweet taste of Sauternes wine with the flavouring from a mild curry powder, transforms common mussels into an exciting, aromatic and flavoursome dish. Serve with some warm Nan bread.

SERVES 4

MUSSELS WITH CURRY JUS AND SAUTERNES

MUSSELS WITH CURRY JUS AND SAUTERNES

1½kg mussels, cleaned, de-bearded and washed well
3 carrots, peeled
4 sticks celery
½ small celeriac, peeled
2 shallots, peeled and very finely diced
50g unsalted butter
2 tablespoons curry powder
250ml Sauternes or similar sweet wine
100ml fresh chicken stock - *see basic 3*
150ml double cream
Squeeze of lemon juice

Cut the carrots, celery and celeriac into 5mm dice.
Cook each separately in salted water and set aside.
In a large, wide-based pan melt the butter and cook the shallots without colouring for 2-3 minutes.
Add the curry powder and cook for one more minute.
Next add the Sauternes wine and reduce by two thirds.
Add the chicken stock next and reduce by half again.
Add the cream and the vegetables and bring to the boil.
Add the mussels, well drained and cover with a lid on high heat.
Shake the pan and stir the mussels to ensure an even cooking until all the mussels are open.
Discard any mussel that does not open.
Finish the dish with a squeeze of fresh lemon juice.
Transfer to a large serving bowl.

Red mullet is an elegant fish. It is found widely in the Mediterranean, but also locally in the warmer summer months. It is classified as a round white fish, but has a richer and more satisfying flavour than most, thanks to its higher fat content. It is sometimes compared to shellfish in taste, and in fact feeds on them. There are two main types of red mullet available in Britain. Both are generally small, and considered best when under 500g in weight. Look for a bright red skin, it has a beautiful appearance and a very fine textured flesh. Unusually for a fish, the red mullet's liver is considered a delicacy in its own right, and that's one reason why mullet are often sold and cooked un-gutted. I use them in the restaurant pounded into a butter which we use to finish a red wine sauce. It's best to use a non-stick frying pan when cooking red mullet. Pan fry in olive oil and allow 2-3 minutes to cook depending on thickness.

SERVES 6

look for a bright red skin...

GRILLED RED MULLET, PEA RISOTTO AND TAPENADE

FOR THE TAPENADE DRESSING:

100g pitted black olives
1 clove garlic, peeled and finely chopped
1 teaspoon thyme leaves, stalks removed
1 anchovy fillet, very finely chopped
150ml olive oil

Place the olives, garlic, thyme and anchovy into a blender or liquidiser.
Turn on the power and drizzle the oil in slowly so it is absorbed by the other ingredients. You will need to scrape down the sides of the bowl occasionally.
Store in the fridge until needed.

FOR THE PEA PURÉE:

300g frozen peas
200ml chicken stock - *see basic 3*
50g butter

Place the peas and stock in a pan with a pinch of salt and cook on a high heat until the peas are tender.
Put the pan contents and the butter into a liquidiser and purée until smooth.
Adjust the seasoning with salt.

FOR THE RISOTTO:

½ onion, finely diced
1 clove garlic, peeled and finely diced
50g unsalted butter
150g Arborio or Carnaroli risotto rice
300-400ml chicken stock, hot - *see basic 3*
50g freshly grated parmesan
12 tablespoons pea purée
Salt and freshly ground white pepper

Melt the butter in a wide-based pan and gently cook the garlic and onion for 2 minutes without colouring.
Add the rice to the pan and stir well to coat the rice with butter.
Add the stock a little at a time, stirring continually so that the rice cooks evenly and does not stick, until it is almost cooked.
Next add the parmesan cheese and the pea purée and mix in well.
Adjust the seasoning with salt and white pepper and set aside.

Note: *To ensure you have a perfectly cooked risotto with no 'bite' to the rice, keep tasting the rice towards the end of the cooking time. You may find you need a little less, or more, stock depending on the heat and size of your pan.*

TO FINISH THE DISH:

12 fillets red mullet, pin-boned and scaled
2 cloves garlic, peeled and very finely sliced
Squeeze lemon juice

Season the fish with salt and place skin side up on a buttered tray.
Top with a couple of garlic slices and place under a hot grill for 2-3 minutes until just cooked.
Season with a squeeze of lemon juice.

TO SERVE:

Divide the risotto between the plates and place two fish fillets on each.
Drizzle the tapenade dressing around the plate and a little on top of the fish.

STEAMED FILLET OF SEA BREAM WITH GLAZED VEGETABLES, STRAW POTATOES AND VINAIGRETTE GOURMANDE

Sea Bream is available throughout the year from many good fishmongers and is particularly delicious steamed. Keep the skin on to help keep it moist, and, when the fish is cooked, simply peel it away using the back of a knife. The straw potatoes, which give this dish a terrific texture, and vinaigrette can be prepared in advance. Cooking the sea bream with vegetables in this way ensures that it is a very simple dish to prepare and serve at a dinner party.

SERVES 6

VINAIGRETTE:

1 tablespoon sherry vinegar
Juice ½ lemon
Pinch salt
Pinch sugar
150ml extra virgin olive oil
2 plum tomatoes, skinned and diced

Put the vinegar, lemon juice, sugar and salt into a bowl and whisk until the solids have dissolved.
Whisk in the olive oil slowly to emulsify it into the liquid.
Stir in the tomato dice and set aside until required.

GLAZED VEGETABLES:

1 carrot
2 courgettes
2 celery stalks
1 bulb fennel
400ml chicken stock - *see basic 3*
1 garlic clove, peeled and cut in half
2 fresh tarragon stems
24 whole chives

Wash and peel the carrot and slice it thinly in 10cm lengths.
Cut each slice into thin strips about the same thickness as the chives.
Do the same with the courgette and celery.
Cut the fennel in half, remove the top and discard.
Break into individual leaves and again slice the same as the carrots.
Put the chicken stock in large wide pan with the garlic and bring it to the boil.
Add the sliced vegetables to the stock and cook for 2-3 minutes so they still have a slight bite to them.
Strain the stock into a clean saucepan, arrange the vegetables on a tray and season them with salt while they are still hot.
Reduce the stock with the tarragon stems, until golden and thick. You should have approximately 100ml of stock in the pan.
Remove the pan from the heat and whisk in the vinaigrette until it's emulsified.

STRAW POTATOES:

500g Maris Piper or Golden Wonder potatoes
Salt

Wash and peel the potatoes.
With the aid of a food processor, shred the potatoes to resemble matchsticks.
Wash again in cold water and then dry by squeezing them in a tea towel to remove all excess moisture.
Deep fry the potatoes a little at a time in vegetable oil at 180°C, turning them with a roasting fork until golden.
Drain on kitchen paper and season with salt.

Note: *These can be served hot or cold*

COOKING THE FISH:

6 fillets of sea bream
100g unsalted butter, melted
Salt
Squeeze lemon juice

Brush the fillets of sea bream with melted butter and season with salt.
Place a portion of the vegetables onto a small plate with 4 chives.
Lay 2 fillets of sea bream on top without overlapping them and cover tightly with cling film.
Place in a steamer. This will only take approximately 10 minutes to cook.

TO SERVE:

Arrange the vegetables and fish in the centre of the plate.
Squeeze a little lemon juice on top of the fish.
Place some of the straw potatoes on top.
Warm the vinaigrette in a pan, add a few chopped chives and then spoon the vinaigrette around the outside.

Note: *You may need to cook the fish in 2 or more batches, depending on the size and capacity of your steamer. If so, you can leave the cling film on the cooked portions for 20 minutes or so to keep warm, until you have cooked the other portions.*

Smoked haddock is a relatively inexpensive and plentiful ingredient. Smoked Finnan haddock is the most famous variety and should always be sold on the bone and with the skin on. Your alternative is to buy smoked haddock fillets - I avoid the bright yellow dyed ones and go for the pale skinned ones. Choose the largest fillets as they tend to taste better with a creamy flavour, and produce larger flakes. The haddock is poached slowly in milk that is flavoured with some shallot and a bay leaf. It will not require long to cook, 5 minutes, depending on thickness, should be plenty, but remember the haddock will continue cooking as it cools down in the milk. This dish is served with braised leeks and a creamy grain mustard sauce, which has a couple of spoonfuls of hollandaise added to it before being spooned onto the plate, and browned under the grill so it turns golden brown. The combination of the flavours does justice to one of our most popular varieties of fish.

SERVES 6

1 quantity braised whole leeks - *see basic 15*

GRATIN OF GRAIN MUSTARD:

2 shallots, peeled and sliced
350ml white wine
350ml fish stock - *see basic 2*
300ml double cream
Hollandaise sauce - *see basic 24*
Grain mustard
Salt
Flat leaf parsley, chopped

Place the shallots and wine in a pan and reduce until the wine is almost completely absorbed.
Add the fish stock and reduce by two thirds.
Add the double cream and bring to the boil. Strain into another pan discarding the shallots.
Reduce this sauce until thick and intensely flavoured.
Mix in a little fresh hollandaise sauce, salt, grain mustard and flat leaf parsley to taste.

TO FINISH:

6 x 120g undyed smoked haddock
500ml milk
1 shallot, peeled and sliced
1 bay leaf
½ lemon

SMOKED HADDOCK WITH BRAISED LEEKS AND A GRAIN MUSTARD SAUCE

In a large pan bring the milk to a simmer with the sliced shallot and bay leaf.
Add the pieces of haddock and poach gently for 5 minutes.
Remove the pan from the heat and leave to rest.

TO SERVE:

On each plate place four spoonfuls of the grain mustard sauce.
Lay the plate under the hot grill for 30-45 seconds or until the sauce starts to turn golden brown turning the plate to finish with an even colour.
Re-heat the braised leeks and when warm place a portion on the centre of each plate.
Gently remove the smoked haddock from the warm milk and lay a portion on top of the leeks, finish with a squeeze of fresh lemon juice and serve immediately.

ROAST MONKFISH
WITH BUTTERED SAVOY CABBAGE, NOILLY PRAT AND CLAMS

Monkfish is especially delicious when poached in Noilly Prat which brings out its slightly sweet flavour. Noilly Prat is a special French dry vermouth excellent for cooking and can be used successfully in many different fish dishes as a replacement for white wine.

Monkfish is a particularly versatile fish to cook with and is low in calories and a good source of protein. The main edible part of the fish is the tail which is how you will usually see it in the fishmongers. Ask him to remove the skin and membrane that covers the beautiful pearly white flesh.

SERVES 6

ROAST MONKFISH WITH BUTTERED SAVOY CABBAGE, NOILLY PRAT AND CLAMS

1 Savoy cabbage
4 shallots
250g unsalted butter, cold and diced
150ml white wine
150ml Noilly Prat
300ml fish stock - *see basic 2*
250ml double cream
36 fresh clams e.g. Venus clams
900g monkfish tail fillets, skinned
Plain flour for dusting
Olive oil
1 lemon
Small bunch flat leaf parsley
Salt

Prepare the cabbage by removing the dark green outer leaves.
Separate the nice green leaves and tear the leafy part into large pieces removing the tough centre vein.
Cook the leaves until just tender in boiling salted water.
Remove from the water and spread out on a wire rack to cool and drain.
Set aside.
Peel and slice the shallots.
Melt 50g of the butter in a pan and add the shallots.
Cook on a gentle heat for 2 minutes without the shallots colouring.
Add the white wine and cook on a high heat until almost completely gone.
Add the Noilly Prat to the pan and cook until reduced by approximately half the volume.
Add the fish stock and reduce by half the volume again.
Strain through a fine sieve into a wide pan and discard the shallots.
Add the cream to the pan and bring to the boil.
Add the clams to the sauce and cook with the lid on until the clams have opened up.
Discard any that are still closed.
Set the sauce aside.
Cut the monkfish into six evenly sized portions and season with salt.
Dust the monkfish lightly in flour and pat it to remove the excess.
Fry the monkfish in a little olive oil on a high heat, turning, until it takes on a golden colour on all sides.
Transfer the monkfish to a tray and cook in the oven at 220°C (Gas mark 7) for 4-6 minutes until the monkfish is just cooked.
Remove from the oven, squeeze a little lemon juice on each piece and set aside in a warm place.
Put 2 tablespoons of water into a wide pan and bring to the boil.
Whisk in the remaining butter until the water and butter has emulsified and add a little salt to taste.
Add the cabbage to the pan to re-heat and coat in the butter emulsion.

TO SERVE:

Divide the cabbage between six bowls and top with the monkfish tails.
Finely shred the parsley leaves and add to the hot sauce with a squeeze of lemon juice and spoon around the cabbage.

This is a simple, healthy and yet satisfying dish to make with contrasting colours and flavours.

There are actually quite a few varieties of beets to choose from other than the common deep purple beets seen in the shops. In the restaurant we use two varieties. The golden beetroot is golden in colour and slightly sweeter to taste while the candy beetroot has defined beautiful pink and white rings through it.

Mackerel is a versatile fish which can be served in a number of ways, for example smoked or pickled, but for this dish I am using freshly grilled mackerel. It is an inexpensive, sustainable and healthy fish and is high in oils and rich in omega-3 fatty acids. It has a robust and strong taste which contrasts well with the sweet beetroot and the acidity of the balsamic vinegar.

SERVES 6

GRILLED MACKEREL WITH A SALAD OF ROASTED BEETROOT, BALSAMIC VINEGAR AND ORGANIC LEAVES

GRILLED MACKEREL WITH A SALAD OF ROASTED BEETROOT, BALSAMIC VINEGAR AND ORGANIC LEAVES

6 medium sized beetroots
200ml extra virgin olive oil
2 sprigs thyme
2 cloves garlic, peeled
9 mint leaves
75ml balsamic vinegar
6 fresh mackerel fillets, pin-bones removed
1 lemon
Salt
Mixed organic leaves e.g. mizuna, red chard, cress, frisée endive

Wash the beetroots well using an abrasive scourer or hard bristled brush and cut into bite sized wedges.
Tear a large piece of kitchen foil and lay it on a flat surface.
Spread the beetroot in a single layer to one side of the foil and season with salt.
Drizzle the beetroot with a little of the olive oil and lay the thyme on top.
Cut the garlic into 3 pieces each and add them to the beets.
Fold the foil over to form an envelope and fold the edges in to seal the bag.
Place in a pre-heated oven at 200°C (Gas mark 6) for 20 minutes or until the beets are cooked fully through.
Remove the garlic and thyme and place the beetroot and its cooking juices into a bowl.
Shred the mint finely and add it to the bowl with the balsamic vinegar and the olive oil and toss together.
Season each side of the mackerel with salt and place on a lightly oiled tray, skin side up.
Drizzle the top of the fish with a little olive oil and place under a hot grill for 2-3 minutes until the fish is just cooked and the skin has started to crisp.
Finish with a squeeze of lemon juice.

TO SERVE:

Divide the beets between six plates.
Whisk the beetroot vinaigrette well and use a little of this to dress your mixed leaves.
Place the leaves on top of the beetroot so that the vegetables are still showing and drizzle a little of the dressing around the plate.
Place the freshly cooked mackerel on top of the salad and serve immediately.

ROAST HALIBUT WITH
ENDIVE AND APPLE SALAD AND SPINACH

This recipe is an adaptation of a recipe my French mother-in-law, Monique, who lives in Mexico City, uses. I have to give the credit for this recipe to Monique, as she prepares this salad every time I visit Mexico City with my wife Cecile. On returning to the UK, I tried it out and wrote the recipe. It is very simple to prepare, but the flavours work really well together, particularly the bitter endive leaves dressed with the oils and sugar. Using raisins, almonds, apple and Roquefort cheese, this is similar in style to a Waldorf salad. I would happily serve all three parts of this dish separately, particularly the spinach which is really delicious served on its own. If you like you can substitute the halibut with salmon, tuna or mackerel. SERVES 4

ENDIVE AND APPLE SALAD WITH ALMONDS, ROQUEFORT AND RAISINS:

1 endive
1 apple
½ espresso spoon of Dijon mustard
20ml white wine vinegar
50ml extra virgin olive oil
25ml almond oil
Pinch sugar
Salt and pepper
50g Roquefort cheese
20 fresh almonds
50g raisins

Cut the endive in half and then cut each half in half again, keeping the shape of the leaf.
Cut the apple in fine slices.
Make a vinaigrette with the mustard, vinegar, olive oil and almond oil, sugar and season.
Cut the Roquefort into small pieces, and mix with the almonds and raisins into the vinaigrette.
Combine with the endive and apple.

COOKING AND SERVING THE FISH:

1 quantity spinach with lemon - *see basic 23*
4 x 120g fillets halibut
Extra virgin olive oil
Salt and pepper

Heat a pan with olive oil and wait until it is extremely hot.
Season the fish with salt on both sides.
Cook the halibut for about one minute on each side, until you get a lovely golden colour on the fish and then finish cooking it in the oven if required.
Place some spinach in the centre of your plate, then the fish and the salad on top.

SEARED PEPPERED TUNA LOIN,
BABY GEM LETTUCE, DRIED TOMATOES
AND A SWEET LEMON DRESSING

This is a perfect summer dish to enjoy with friends and family and is simple and easy to prepare. Tuna is an excellent source of lean protein, vitamins and minerals and is a wonderful way to excite the palate while eating healthily. However, tuna has more to offer than just great taste and nutrition. Tuna can also help lower blood pressure and cholesterol. Research has shown that omega-3 fatty acids - found in abundance in oily fish like tuna - can help lower the risk of heart disease.

A sweet lemon dressing is the perfect accompaniment to this dish. The custom of serving a slice of lemon with fish dates back to the Middle Ages. It was believed that if a person accidentally swallowed a fish bone, the lemon juice would dissolve it. Nowadays we tend to incorporate lemon flavours because they enhance the taste of fish. In this recipe I have used lemon grass, a main ingredient in Thai and south-east Asian cuisines. Lemon grass is a pale green stalk that can be used fresh, dried or powdered to impart its lemon flavour to sweet or savoury dishes. It's not exactly a lemon flavour, but the strong scent is noticeably citrus. Fresh stalks are sold in many supermarkets and will keep in the fridge for about a week.

SERVES 6

SEARED PEPPERED TUNA LOIN, BABY GEM LETTUCE, DRIED TOMATOES AND A SWEET LEMON DRESSING

9 tomatoes, ripe but firm
Maldon sea salt
Caster sugar
2 cloves garlic
1 sprig thyme
1 stick lemongrass, bashed
2 tablespoons white wine vinegar
1 tablespoon brown sugar
2 tablespoons lemon juice
6 tablespoons peanut oil
4 tablespoons olive oil
6 tablespoons black peppercorns
600g trimmed tuna loin, whole piece
3 Baby Gem lettuce

FOR THE TOMATOES:

Cut a small cross in the bottom of the tomatoes and peel them by first dropping them into a pan of boiling water for 30 seconds and then straight into a bowl of iced water.
Remove the skin and cut the tomatoes vertically into quarters.
Cut out and discard the seeds to leave you with the flesh.
Place the tomatoes in a bowl with a pinch each of salt and sugar and a drizzle of olive oil.
Toss gently to coat.
Arrange the tomatoes on a cooling or cake rack and top with the garlic peeled and cut into very thin slices.
Leave the tomatoes in a warm place or an oven at 70°C until lightly dried.
This will take 60-90 minutes.

FOR THE DRESSING:

Place the thyme, lemon grass, vinegar and brown sugar in a small pan and heat gently, whisking until the sugar has dissolved.
Allow to cool.
Whisk this mix together with the lemon juice and oils and season with a pinch of salt.

TO FINISH THE DISH:

Crush the peppercorns well with the base of a saucepan into evenly sized pieces.
Roll the tuna in the peppercorns to coat evenly and season with Maldon sea salt crushed lightly between your fingers.
Fry the tuna in a hot pan with olive oil for about 30 seconds on each side, the tuna should still be very pink.
Remove from the pan.
Place the Baby Gem leaves in a bowl with the tomatoes and coat with the dressing which has been whisked well.
Divide evenly between the plates and top with the sliced tuna loin.

my favourite fish

JOHN DORY WITH CREAMED BRUSSELS SPROUTS

John Dory has to be one of my favourite fish to eat. It's best pan-fried as it has a good firm texture to it. It is, however, one of the harder varieties of fish to fillet as it has sharp needles in the spine and close to the gills. It's a good idea to ask the fishmonger to fillet it for you. Although Brussels sprouts are seasonal, it's worth trying to cook them this way and I have not tasted a better way to eat them!

SERVES 6

JOHN DORY WITH CREAMED BRUSSELS SPROUTS

150g carrot
150g celeriac
120g unsmoked bacon
100g unsalted butter
450g Brussels sprouts
500ml chicken stock - *see basic 3*
300ml double cream
6 fillets of John Dory
Olive oil for frying
1 lemon
Salt

Cut the carrot and celeriac into 2mm dice and set aside.
Cut the bacon into thin lardons (strips).
Melt the butter in a wide, heavy-based pan and fry the lardons until starting to brown.
Add the carrot and celeriac to the pan and cook for 2 minutes.
Cut the sprouts in half and remove the outer leaves and tough core.
Shred the sprouts finely and add to the pan.
Cook for 1 minute turning to coat in the butter and season lightly with salt.
Heat the chicken stock in a pan and add it to the sprouts.
Cook on a high heat until the stock has reduced almost completely and the sprouts are almost cooked.
Add the cream and cook on a high heat to reduce to a thick consistency. Set aside.
Remove the skin from the fish and separate the fillets, removing the frill on the very edge.
Fry the fillets on a medium to high heat in the olive oil until golden brown on both sides and just cooked.
Remove from the pan and season with a squeeze of lemon juice.

TO SERVE:

Divide the sprouts between six plates and place the fish on top.
Serve immediately with buttered new potatoes or spätzle - *see basic 14*

In this dish the sea bass has been steamed as it's a great way to keep the true flavour of the fish. I don't tend to use a lot of Asian Pacific style ingredients in my cooking at the restaurant, but I do enjoy eating them. It's useful to cook with different styles of soya sauce which can vary in flavour and change with maturity. Wild bass is best for this although a good sized farmed sea bass fillet will work as well.

SERVES 6

STEAMED WILD SEA BASS WITH SPRING ONION, GINGER AND SOY

6 x 120g sea bass portions, skin on and scaled
2 bunches spring onions
5cm piece ginger
1 tablespoon ketjap manis (sweet soy sauce)
3 tablespoons light soy sauce
2 tablespoons sesame oil
1 lime
1 bunch coriander leaf
Thick noodles (e.g. Udon noodles)

Get your fishmonger to prepare your sea bass fillets by removing the pin bones and scaling the fillets.
Cut the sides into appropriate portion sizes of approximately 120-150g each.
Cut the spring onions in half lengthways and then cut into 3mm dice.
Place them in a mixing bowl.
Peel the ginger and slice it very thinly, 1-2mm, either by hand or on a slicer.
Cut each slice into 2mm strips lengthways and then cut each strip across into 2mm dice.
Add this to the bowl.
Add the ketjap manis and the light soy to the bowl and whisk in the sesame oil to combine.
Add lime juice to taste and whisk in.
Tear off a piece of kitchen foil and spoon some of the ginger / soy mix onto it.
Lightly season your bass fillet with salt and place on top of the dressing.
Fold the foil over the fish and seal the edges to form an airtight envelope.
Repeat with all of the fish.
Place the bag in a stove top steamer for 9-12 minutes depending on the thickness of the fish until just cooked.

TO SERVE:

Open up the bag and lift the fish out onto a plate.
Carefully remove the skin.
When the fish is perfectly cooked the skin will peel back easily.
Spoon the cooking juices over the top of the fish.
Finely shred (chiffonade) the coriander leaf and sprinkle it over the fish and serve it with some cooked thick noodles.

Vermouth, which is essentially a white wine that's been infused with a careful balance of spice and herbs, is a fantastic aperitif served chilled. However, reduce it in a pan and add a little home-made fish stock, and you have the most wonderful base to poach a beautiful piece of fish in. The addition of more flavour, by adding a little mustard and some fresh herbs at the end, finish off a remarkably easy dish to cook.

SERVES 6

POACHED MONKFISH WITH VERMOUTH, GRAIN MUSTARD, FRESH TAGLIATELLE PASTA AND YOUNG SPINACH

POACHED MONKFISH WITH VERMOUTH, GRAIN MUSTARD, FRESH TAGLIATELLE PASTA AND YOUNG SPINACH

1 quantity pasta - *see basic 13*

ROLLING AND COOKING THE PASTA:

Roll out the pasta as thin as you can (using a pasta machine) then cut into thin even strips using a sharp knife.

Place the pasta into boiling salted water; it will only take 30 seconds to cook.

When ready, cool down under running water.

Drain the water off and mix with a little olive oil and set aside until you are ready to serve.

250g unsalted butter, cold and diced
2 shallots, peeled and sliced
1 clove of garlic, peeled and sliced
100ml Vermouth
200ml fish stock - *see basic 2*
6 x 120g portions of monkfish tails
50ml double cream
1 tablespoon grain mustard
1 tomato, diced
2 tablespoons parsley, finely chopped
1 lemon
250g young spinach leaves, washed
Salt and freshly ground white pepper

PREPARING THE STOCK:

Melt 15g of the butter in a large saucepan and sweat the shallot and garlic to soften but do not allow them to colour.

Add the Vermouth and reduce until the liquid has virtually evaporated.

Add the fish stock and reduce the volume by half.

Remove the stock from the heat and set aside until you are ready to cook the fish.

PREPARING AND COOKING THE FISH:

Bring the reduced stock to simmering point in a pan.

Place the fillets on a chopping board and season with a little salt.

Place the fish into the pan and cover immediately with a tight-fitting lid.

Allow the fish to poach for 3-5 minutes on a medium heat, depending on the thickness of the fillets.

Remove the fish from the pan and place it on a warm plate.

Cover the plate tightly with cling film to keep the fish warm and moist.

FINISHING THE SAUCE:

Strain the stock through a fine sieve into a small saucepan.

Reduce the stock until there is only 100ml remaining.

Add the double cream to the pan and bring it to the boil.

Whisk in the remaining diced butter a little at a time over a low heat being careful not to let it boil and separate.

Finally add the grain mustard, diced tomato, chopped parsley and a few drops of lemon juice.

TO SERVE:

Gently sauté the spinach in a pan with a little butter and place some in the centre of a warm plate.

Re-heat the pasta in a pan of simmering water for 30 seconds and drain into a bowl.

Season the pasta with salt and freshly ground white pepper, then place some on top of the spinach.

Using a sharp knife, slice the monkfish and arrange it around the pasta.

Spoon the sauce over the top of the fish and pasta and serve immediately.

POACHED FILLETS OF LEMON SOLE WITH LANGOUSTINE TAILS AND CITRUS FENNEL, VEGETABLE AND HERB NAGE

I cook this dish a lot at home as it is a very fresh and light dish to eat. The citrus fennel is delicious and can also be served with grilled tuna or is perfect for the long, lazy summer evenings as an accompaniment to barbecued chicken.

Vegetable nage (or stock) is one of the most useful stocks to have on hand and is very healthy and inexpensive. It is simple to make and the ingredients are available all year round. The best results are obtained using freshly cut vegetables and herbs. SERVES 6

POACHED FILLETS OF LEMON SOLE WITH LANGOUSTINE TAILS AND CITRUS FENNEL, VEGETABLE AND HERB NAGE

1 quantity vegetable nage: *Make one day in advance* - *see basic 6*

1 quantity citrus fennel - *see basic 20*

LANGOUSTINE TAILS:

12 langoustines

Separate the tails from the langoustines and remove the intestinal tract by twisting the base of the tail and pulling.

Cook langoustine tails in boiling salted water for 40 seconds, remove from the water.

Remove the hard shell from the langoustine tails and set the meat aside for finishing the dish.

TO FINISH AND SERVE THE DISH:

6 lemon sole fillets, skinned

1 clove garlic

1 sprig tarragon

¼ cucumber, peeled and diced

Vegetable nage

1 tablespoon soy sauce

Lemon

Cut the sole fillets in half lengthways and arrange them in a wide-based saucepan to fit snugly in one layer.

Put the langoustines, garlic and tarragon on top of the fish.

Cover with some of the vegetable nage and cook the fish gently, not allowing it to boil, until the sole fillets are a clean white colour.

Re-heat the fennel and place a spoonful in the centre of a soup plate.

Place two pieces of sole and a couple of langoustines on top of the fennel.

Add the soy sauce, cucumber and lemon juice to the vegetable nage and pour it over the fish.

The Michelin star

"Ca Marche! Two Covers!"

At the height of Saturday evening dinner service the Head Waiter bursts into the kitchen and pins a new order on the pass. Three white rectangular plates are already warming on this electric hot-plate and steel work surface, which marks the territorial divide between the bustling kitchen and the controlled calm of the restaurant beyond.

Four spotlights blaze down on an empty porcelain triptych, a blank canvas on which Martin Wishart is about to create. He grabs the new order and announces it to the kitchen. *"Starters: one Tuna, one Foie Gras. Mains: one Dory, one Soufflé."* Four simple headlines but enough to galvanize eight lieutenant chefs into action. Within minutes each will deliver crucial components to create the elaborate à la carte dishes.

For now concentration is back on the pass, as the three tasting menu plates begin to be composed. Elegant rows of perfectly turned Vivaldi potatoes, interspersed with fine spears of asparagus all placed at the same oblique angles; a delicate but licentious piping of crème fraîche. Next the star ingredient: Scottish East Coast squid which has been scored when raw and flat, and now arrives in tight seductive curls from its momentary pan fried cooking. Then for texture, three sands of malt, pumpernickel and truffle are crumbled between Martin's fingers to give the perfect finish to each plate. Time seems to freeze as the Chef appraises his creation, the very instant when a skilled photographer would release the shutter. Then a commanding: *"Away!"* as waiters' hands swoop in.

The pressure in a Michelin-starred kitchen is relentless. Fortunately, skills are so practised they also become automatic. The knack is to be energised, but not carried away, by the adrenaline, and everyone must find ways of keeping themselves under control. Forcing oneself to breathe evenly, and projecting oneself momentarily into an imaginary and tranquil place can certainly help.

One such place for Martin was a real beach at Puerto Escondido in Mexico on a perfect summer's evening. The sun low in the sky, the calming sound of gentle waves lapping the sand and the Chef and his soon to be wife finding themselves at an impromptu beach café. A welcoming local woman came out from her hut holding perfectly fresh Pacific red snapper and offering to cook. She then disappeared into her tiny

kitchen, and later presented the fish in the most simple way, but also with the most warm and endearing smile. For Martin, it is reassuring to be reminded that the best culinary experience comes down to these fundamentals. Excellent fresh ingredients, perfect cooking, simple and friendly service.

"Three minutes to soufflé!" a junior pastry chef updates the main kitchen before dashing back to supervise the soufflé oven. As soon as he speaks a timer is switched on, giving a relentless countdown to the moment when the two à la carte main courses must leave the pass. All minds must now be focused on the split-second timing involved in delivering their components. In the base of the large soufflé bowl, succulent cuts of gently poached lobster and smoked haddock are already

prepared, basking under the hot lights. A paysanne of leeks cooked in rich butter forms the base of the John Dory plate, where tender fillets of the most ferociously ugly, yet flavoursome of fish, will soon come to rest.

Two minutes and counting. A round lattice of crispy potato is placed on top of the leeks and the plate geometrically garnished with golden raisins and three mussels in their shells, fresh from the oven and oozing with a gratin of chopped almond and Parmesan cheese. A sous chef has two sauce pans at the ready, one a rich lobster for the soufflé, the other a stunning combination of aromatic curry spices and Sauternes dessert wine. Both need to be buzzed almost simultaneously to create the frothy, savoury cappuccinos that Martin will need.

One minute and counting. Two waiters are poised, focusing intently on every final stage of the process. Nervous about acting at exactly the right moment, but trying not to show it. The soufflé arrives and to everyone's relief is successfully turned out of its ramekin and on to the waiting plate. A final flash under the grill when one can see and smell the lobster coral butter it has been cooked in, turn golden orange on top. The crisp John Dory fillets are put perfectly in place. The soufflé comes down, is sauced, then instantly dispatched. The curry and Sauternes foam is delicately spooned onto the Dory and sent.

The plates arrive at the table simultaneously. The waiter's attention subtly shifting from the concentration needed to

place the plate correctly, to the irresistible urge to measure the reaction on the guests' faces. Another instant when time stands still. The look of delight when they see a perfectly risen soufflé. The moment when the rich aroma of the curry and Sauternes rises off the plate and assaults the senses.

Ecstatic anticipation of pleasure.

rom farm to fork, people these days just love to know exactly where their meat is oming from. Do buy the best quality you can afford, as the extra cost will ultimately reward ou and your guests with an abundance of extra flavour. In here you'll find recipes using neat, game and poultry, based on what I like to cook at home and which take into account easonal availability and styles of meat you may not have tried before.

Meat

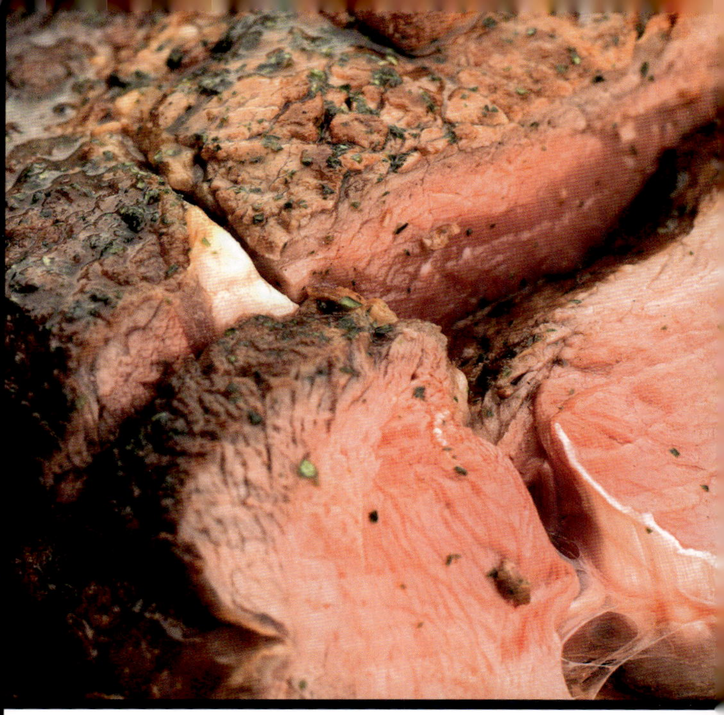

This whole roast duck dish with spices and crispy coating of home-made gingerbread will fill your kitchen with a mouth-watering aroma. Use freshly bought five spices or better still buy the spices whole and crush to a powder using a pestle and mortar. The five spices are: star anise, cinnamon, cloves, fennel seed and Sichuan peppercorns.

During the winter I often serve this dish at my restaurant as a sharing dish for two. The legs can be used for confit and served with a salad. The Pont Neuf potatoes, which are a large cut chip, do take a little time to prepare and cook, but the texture and taste remind me of the ones my Mum would cook for us when I was a boy and are so much better than those pre-cut varieties that take up rows of supermarket freezer space. Go on, give them a try!

You need to start preparing this dish the day before you want to eat it. Begin by making the pain d'épices - French gingerbread, and then prepare the duck, so the spices have time to penetrate the meat. Then, the next day, all you have to do is cook the duck, prepare the salad, and of course, cook the chips.

SERVES 6-8

ROAST GRESSINGHAM DUCK COATED IN FRENCH GINGERBREAD, WHITE RADISH SALAD AND POMMES PONT NEUF

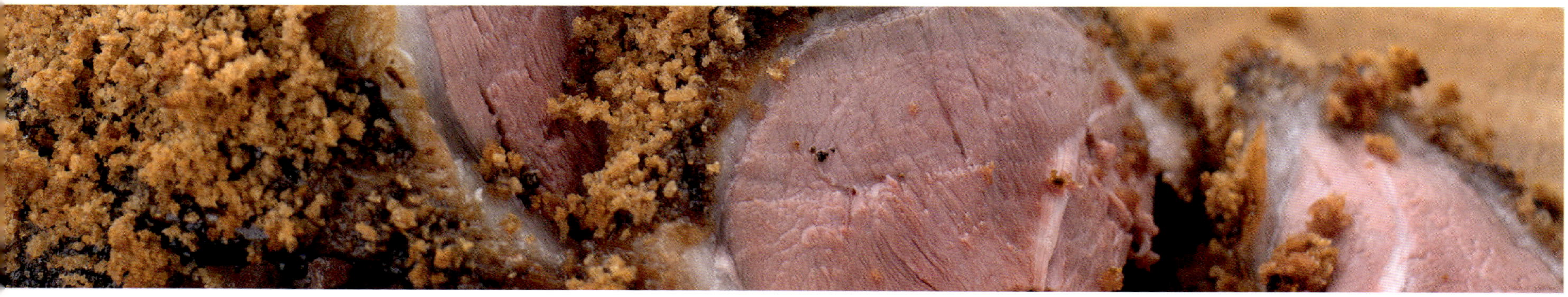

PAIN D'ÉPICES:

250ml honey
125ml milk
Zest ½ lemon
Zest ½ orange
1 vanilla pod, seeds only
3 eggs
50g caster sugar
120g rye flour
120g plain flour
20g mixed spice
Pinch ground cinnamon

Warm the milk and honey together in a pan.
Mix in the zests and vanilla seeds.
Put the eggs and sugar into a large bowl and whisk to a light and fluffy sabayon over a pan of boiling water.
Sieve together the spices and flours.
Fold together the sabayon, flours and liquid mix.
Pour into terrine moulds lined with silicone paper.
Bake at 160°C (Gas mark 3) for approximately 45 minutes, or until a knife comes out cleanly.
Cool on a wire rack.

PREPARING THE DUCK:

2 Gressingham ducks 1.5-1.7kg each
30g Chinese five spice
20g caster sugar
Salt and pepper
100ml honey

Remove the legs and wings and reserve for another recipe (i.e. duck confit).
With a sharp knife, score diagonally across the duck skin to expose the meat.
Dust with the five spice and sugar, rubbing well into the skin.
Cover with cling film and refrigerate for 24 hours.

THE NEXT DAY...

COOKING THE DUCK:

Pre-heat the oven to 200°C (Gas mark 6). Season the duck with salt and pepper, colour each side until golden brown in a pan on top of the stove, then transfer into the oven and cook for 30-35 minutes.
Slice the gingerbread and blend in a food processor to make coarse breadcrumbs.
When the ducks are ready, remove from the oven and allow them to rest for 10 minutes.
Warm the honey and pour it onto the duck breast, sprinkle with the ginger bread and press down to create a thick crust.
Place ducks back in the oven for another 10 minutes so the ginger bread crust can crisp.

Cook the chips in the fryer at 140°C until just done (soft in the centre) and lightly coloured. The chips can be left like this well in advance and finished when required.
To finish, increase the fryer temperature to 180 / 190°C and cook the chips until crispy and golden.
Remove onto paper towel and season appropriately with salt.

TO FINISH THE DISH AND SERVE:

200g mixed salad leaves
300g white radish, peeled
1 lemon
Pinch sugar
3 tablespoons olive oil
Salt and pepper

Thinly slice the white radish and mix with the lemon juice, sugar and olive oil, season with a little salt and allow it to marinade for 10 minutes.
Add the mixed salad leaves and mix together.
Take the whole ducks to the table and carve them in front of your guests.
Serve with the pommes Pont Neuf and salad.

PONT NEUF POTATOES:

12 large floury potatoes (Golden Wonder)
Deep fat fryer pre-heated to 140°C.

Wash the potatoes well and peel.
Cut them into even-sized chips of 7cm length with a square cross-section of about 1½cm.
Allow 9 chips per person (with a few spare to test!).
Half cook the chips in boiling salted water.
Remove from water carefully with a slotted spoon and place onto a wire rack to steam dry for 5 minutes.

ROAST ORGANIC CHICKEN STUFFED WITH HERB BRIOCHE, SERVED WITH BRAISED LEEKS, GRATIN OF POTATOES, PARSLEY AND WHITE WINE GRAVY

I recommend buying organic or free-range chickens which are naturally grain fed and nutritious - high in protein, low in fat and richer in flavour too. One of the best ways to further intensify the flavour is to stuff the skin of the bird. I like to use a stuffing made with brioche mixed with butter, garlic and fresh aromatic herbs, I use tarragon which goes really well with poultry. Brioche is a French bread, which is enriched with egg and butter to give it a rich and tender crumb; this also gives the stuffing a wonderful texture. The reason I choose to stuff the skin of the chicken instead of the cavity, is so the stuffing flavours can permeate the meat and ensure the meat retains more moisture and succulent juices during cooking. To accompany the roast chicken I have chosen a potato gratin, adding seasonality by using braised leeks. The creamy richness of the gratin adds contrast to the white meat with white wine gravy trickled over and a sprinkling of parsley to serve.

SERVES 6-8

ROAST ORGANIC CHICKEN STUFFED WITH HERB BRIOCHE, SERVED WITH BRAISED LEEKS, GRATIN OF POTATOES, PARSLEY AND WHITE WINE GRAVY

PREPARING THE CHICKEN:

200g brioche loaf, crusts removed and roughly diced
250g unsalted butter, softened
20g tarragon, leaves picked
10g parsley, chopped
1 clove garlic, finely chopped
Salt
2 medium-sized organic chickens

Place brioche into a food processor with the herbs, garlic and softened butter and blend to a coarse paste.
Add salt to taste and transfer to a piping bag. Keep at room temperature.
Remove the legs and wing tips from the chicken and the undercarriage (bottom of the rib cage) to leave the crown with the breasts on, being careful not to damage the skin.
From the neck (the fat part of the breasts) open a small gap between the meat and the skin and pipe in a large knob of the brioche mix smoothing through the skin with your fingers until evenly spread. Do this on both breasts.
Lightly oil and season the chicken and place on a tray in an oven pre-heated to 200°C (Gas mark 6) and cook for 30-40 minutes. The skin should be golden brown.
Remove from the oven and allow the meat to rest for 10 minutes.

PARSLEY AND WHITE WINE GRAVY:

150ml white wine
200ml double cream
1 teaspoon Dijon mustard
3 tablespoons parsley, chopped

Remove any fat from the roasting tray and discard.
Add the wine to the tray and reduce on top of the stove by half.
Then add the cream and boil for 1-2 minutes.
Whisk in the Dijon mustard and then pass the sauce through a fine sieve into a clean pan, add the chopped parsley and check the seasoning.

GRATIN OF POTATOES:

1kg potatoes, peeled and thinly sliced
5g salt
250ml milk
400ml double cream
2 cloves garlic, sliced
1 tablespoon ground nutmeg

Arrange the potatoes in a well buttered dish to a depth of about 2 inches.
Put the milk, cream, garlic, salt and nutmeg into a pan and bring it up to the boil.
Strain this liquid over the potatoes while hot.
Dot the top of the potatoes with butter.
Cook in a pre-heated oven at 220°C (Gas mark 7) for around 50 minutes. If the potatoes start to turn too dark they can be covered with kitchen foil towards the end of the cooking.

TO SERVE:

500g French beans cooked in boiling, salted water until tender.
1 quantity braised leeks - *see basic 15*

Arrange the chickens, leeks and French beans on a warm serving dish and take to the table to carve in front of your guests.
Serve the potatoes and gravy on the side.

find a large brick...

This recipe requires a good quality free-range or organic chicken, a large heavy-based pan and one clean, heavy stone or brick - which you wrap in tin foil and pre-heat in the oven before cooking your chicken. I know it sounds a little strange but it works perfectly well. A traditional Tuscan dish, pollo al mattone, employs this method, the brick on top keeps it flat and ensures an even cooking and a good amount of crisp skin.

Marinading the bird overnight in olive oil, thyme, lemon and garlic increases the incredible flavours of this roast chicken and makes a great family meal.

SERVES 4

1 organic or free-range chicken (1.5kg)
2 lemons
3 cloves garlic
1 teaspoon black peppercorns, coarsely crushed
1 small bunch fresh thyme
50ml olive oil
Sea salt
Stones or bricks

Cut the chicken in half along the backbone, then through the breastbone.
Cut one and a half lemons into slices, reserving the other half for serving with the cooked chicken.
Peel and roughly chop the garlic and mix in a large bowl with the crushed peppercorns, thyme, olive oil and a good pinch of sea salt.
Add the chicken halves and cover them with the olive oil marinade, cling film the bowl and leave in the fridge for 24 hours.

THE NEXT DAY...

COOKING THE CHICKEN:

Pre-heat the oven to 200°C (Gas mark 6).
Wrap the heavy stones or bricks in tin foil, and place in oven to heat.
Heat a large heavy-based pan, which is big enough to fit both the chicken halves, on the stove over a high heat with 2 tablespoons of olive oil.
When the pan is very hot place the chicken halves skin side down in the pan.
Cover with a couple of pieces of lemon and thyme and place the stones on top.
Cook on the stove for 5-10 minutes until they are uniformly golden brown, then place in the oven and cook for 20 minutes.
Turn the chicken halves over, replacing the stones or bricks on top, and cook for a further 20 minutes.

TO SERVE:

Place the chicken halves on a large platter, squeeze the juice from the reserved half lemon and drizzle with some olive oil over the top and serve.

ORGANIC CRISP CHICKEN WITH LEMON, GARLIC AND THYME COOKED UNDER A BRICK

ROASTED SADDLE OF FRENCH FARMED RABBIT SERVED WITH YOUNG LEEKS, ASPARAGUS, MUSHROOM AND HERB RISOTTO AND A TOMATO AND WHITE WINE JUS

A good quality farmed or wild rabbit can make a wonderfully tasty dish. Its flavour is a little stronger than chicken but is not as intense as game. Rabbit can be cooked in much the same way as chicken, and many chicken recipes can be adapted for rabbit. It goes particularly well with intense flavours such as mustard, garlic, herbs, wine and bacon. This particular recipe incorporates a delicious mushroom risotto, asparagus and leeks which give the dish a wealth of flavour.

SERVES 4

FOR THE RISOTTO:

50g unsalted butter
1 clove garlic, peeled and finely diced
150g white button mushrooms, finely chopped
½ onion, finely diced
150g Arborio or Carnaroli risotto rice
300-400ml hot chicken stock - *see basic 3*
50g freshly grated parmesan
75g mascarpone cheese
Salt and freshly ground white pepper

Melt the butter in a wide-based pan and gently cook the garlic, mushrooms and onion for 2 minutes without colouring.
Add the rice to the pan and stir well to coat the rice with butter.
Add the stock a little at a time, stirring continually so that the rice cooks evenly and does not stick, until it is almost cooked.
Next add the parmesan and mascarpone cheese and mix in well.
Adjust the seasoning with salt and white pepper and set aside.

Note: *To ensure you have a perfectly cooked risotto with no 'bite' to the rice, keep tasting the rice towards the end of the cooking time. You may find you need a little less, or more, stock depending on the heat and size of your pan.*

THE SAUCE:

4 saddles of rabbit, bones removed and reserved
Olive oil
1 carrot, peeled and chopped
1 small onion, peeled and chopped
1 clove garlic, peeled and chopped
1 stick celery, chopped
1 tomato, chopped

ROASTED SADDLE OF FRENCH FARMED RABBIT SERVED WITH YOUNG LEEKS, ASPARAGUS, MUSHROOM AND HERB RISOTTO AND A TOMATO AND WHITE WINE JUS

200ml white wine
300ml chicken stock - *see basic 3*
400ml double cream
Salt and freshly ground white pepper

Chop the bones into 2cm pieces.
Sauté them in one tablespoon of olive oil using a heavy-bottomed saucepan on top of the stove until golden brown, then drain off any excess fat.
Add all the prepared vegetables to the pan and sauté for 4-5 minutes until they also turn golden brown.
Add the white wine to the pan and reduce by two thirds.
Next add the chicken stock and reduce this by two thirds.
Pour the double cream into the sauce and bring to the boil, then simmer for 3-4 minutes.
Pass the sauce through a fine sieve, using the aid of a wooden spoon to extract all the juice from the bones, into a small, clean saucepan.
The sauce will need seasoning with a little salt and white pepper, then place aside until ready to use.

TO FINISH THE DISH AND SERVE:

4 saddles of rabbit (the 8 loins removed from preparing the sauce)
16 fresh asparagus spears, peeled
12 baby leeks, washed and trimmed
1 small sprig fresh tarragon, chopped
Flesh of one tomato, diced
Salt
Olive oil for frying

Heat a large sauté pan, then add one tablespoon of olive oil.
Season the rabbit loins with salt and fry in the pan, turning the pieces until they are golden brown and cooked through. This will take about 8-10 minutes in total.
While the rabbit is cooking, cook the asparagus and leeks in salted boiling water for 3-4 minutes then drain and leave aside to keep warm.
Lay out four warm plates and place the risotto in the centre of each.
Finely slice the rabbit and arrange on top of the risotto.
Lay the asparagus and the baby leeks around the outside of the rabbit, warm the sauce, adding the tarragon and diced tomato, and pour over the vegetables.

CULZEAN PARTRIDGE WITH RUMBLE-DE-THUMPS

A close relative to the pheasant, partridge comes in several varieties, the most popular being the red leg. It is a beautiful small bird and a whole one will feed one person. It has a sweet tasty meat which develops a stronger flavour if hung correctly (3-4 days) by any game dealer or butcher. As it is a seasonally shot bird, it is best to buy fresh partridge between September and the end of January. Roasting is the best method of cooking and here it is served with mashed potatoes, cabbage and onions otherwise known as Rumble-de-thumps, a recipe which hails from the Scottish borders.

SERVES 4

CULZEAN PARTRIDGE
WITH RUMBLE-DE-THUMPS

POTATO AND CABBAGE RUMBLE-DE-THUMPS:

500g Yukon Gold potatoes
500g Savoy cabbage or spring cabbage
1 medium sized onion
50g unsalted butter
1 tablespoon chives, chopped
Salt and pepper

Peel the potatoes and boil in salted water.
When cooked, strain off the water and mash them with a potato masher.
Finely slice the cabbage and boil in salted water for 3-5 minutes until tender.
Refresh under cold water and squeeze out any moisture.
Finely slice the onions and melt the butter in a heavy-based saucepan.
Add the onions and cook over a low heat for 30-45 minutes until they are caramelised and golden brown in colour.
Mix the potato purée, cabbage, onions and chives together.
Season with salt and pepper.
Place in a serving dish brushed with some melted butter and place under a hot grill until golden brown.

THE PARTRIDGES:

4 dressed partridges
250g of mixed wild mushrooms (Black Trompettes, Hedgehog, Chanterelle, Porcini, Morels, Portobello etc)
50g butter
Salt

Heat a little oil in a casserole pan.
Season the partridges with salt and brown them lightly in the oil.
Place the partridges on a tray and cook in the oven at 210°C (Gas mark 6) for 8-10 minutes.
When cooked, remove the birds from the oven and rest them for 10-15 minutes in a warm place before serving.

TO SERVE:

Place the partridges on a serving plate.
Season the wild mushrooms with salt and sauté in butter until golden brown.
Arrange the mushrooms around each partridge.
Serve with the rumble-de-thumps.

surprisingly plump and tender...

Quail are generally sold in oven-ready condition requiring no real preparation and are sold as complete birds. Don't be misled by their tiny appearance, which is in fact quite deceptive as they are surprisingly plump and tender. For the best results roast them whole, serving two birds for a main course portion. This recipe is suitable both as a starter and a main course, depending on the number of birds used. The roast quail is served with a walnut and grape vinaigrette which is made with a mixture of different oils. Peeling the walnuts and grapes is a little time-consuming, but removing the tough skin improves the flavour.

SERVES 3 OR 6 AS A STARTER

ROAST QUAIL WITH WALNUTS AND GRAPE VINAIGRETTE

4 tablespoons peanut oil (groundnut oil)
2 tablespoons extra virgin olive oil
2 tablespoons walnut oil
1 tablespoon sherry vinegar
Pinch salt
Pinch sugar
36 shelled walnut halves
Milk
36 green seedless grapes
6 small oven-ready quail
Vegetable oil for frying

Place the oils, vinegar, salt and sugar into a bowl and whisk to dissolve the solids.
Put the walnuts into a pan and cover with cold milk.
Bring to the boil and simmer for 1 minute.
Remove from the heat and allow to cool slightly.
Peel the skin from the walnuts using the pointed tip of a small knife.
Peel the skin from the grapes and cut in half lengthways.
Season the quail inside and out with salt and colour in a heavy-based pan in a little vegetable oil.
Transfer the quail to an oven tray and place in a pre-heated oven at 220°C (Gas mark 7) for 10 to 15 minutes.
Remove the quail from the oven and allow to rest in a warm place for 10 minutes.

TO SERVE:

Place the quail on 3 plates and pour the juices into the vinaigrette.
Whisk the vinaigrette well to emulsify the liquids and stir in the grapes and walnuts.
Spoon the vinaigrette around the birds, distributing the nuts and grapes evenly between the plates.

Note: *The bird will be cooked slightly pink in this recipe and so will remain moist and delicate.*

As a Scottish chef, the quality of our beef is something that I am very proud of. I have worked with Scottish beef in almost every kitchen that I have worked in, and with first hand knowledge I am proud to know that many top chefs around the world use Scottish beef in their restaurant kitchens. Our climate provides the perfect conditions for cattle rearing and thanks to our farmers and the people involved in Quality Meat Scotland, based in Newbridge, who are responsible for the integrity and reputation of Scotch Beef and lamb, traceability is now a necessity for chefs and the public, providing us with the knowledge of exactly where the beef we use was raised. I always recommend that you go to a well respected butcher when buying beef and this particular cut is best if hung for approximately 28 days. A good 'marbling' of fat and a dark, rich red colour are the two key visual points to look for.

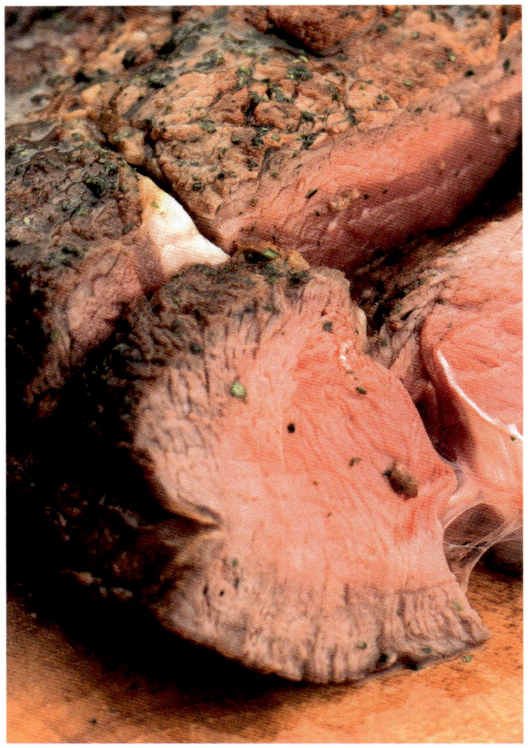

ROAST RIB OF BEEF WITH FRENCH BEANS, ROASTED ARTICHOKE AND POMMES SAUTÉES LYONNAISES

Serving this dish with the French beans, artichokes and pommes sautées Lyonnaises mixed together not only gives a wonderful flavour and texture, but also means that everyone can help themselves from the one platter. This dish is one that I have been serving at my restaurant since I opened it back in 1999 and is still requested by many of my regulars today.

SERVES 4

FRENCH BEANS:

200g fine French beans

Remove the tops and tails of the beans.
Bring a pan of well salted water to the boil and cook the beans for 5 minutes or until just done.
Remove from the water and toss in a little soft butter until well coated.

THE ARTICHOKES:

½ a globe artichoke per person
1 lemon
1 bay leaf
1 sprig fresh thyme
1 tablespoon white wine vinegar
8 white peppercorns
2 tablespoons plain flour

Remove the outer leaves of the artichoke and break off the stalk.
Cut the base flat then neatly trim the outside of the artichoke and rub with lemon to prevent discolouration.
Bring a pan of salted water to the boil with the bay leaf, fresh thyme, white peppercorns, white wine vinegar and the juice of half a lemon.
Whisk in a paste made from the plain flour and half a cup of cold water.
Cook the artichokes in this liquid until just done, remove from the heat and allow them to cool in the liquid.
When cool, remove the firm 'heart' of the choke carefully with a spoon.
Cut the artichokes into 8 or 12 triangular pieces each and dry on kitchen paper.

POMMES SAUTÉES LYONNAISES:

30-40 new potatoes, peeled
50g unsalted butter
4 large onions, peeled and thinly sliced
Salt

Cook the potatoes until done in boiling salted water. Drain and allow them to cool, then cut them in half.
Melt the butter in a heavy-based pan and add the onions and a pinch of salt.
Cook over a medium to low heat stirring constantly until the onions take on a golden brown colour. This will take some time and the onions should be sweet.
Remove to a suitable container to cool.
Chop through the onions lightly once cooled.
Sauté the potatoes in olive oil until golden brown.
Stir through the cooked onions and set aside.

ROAST RIB OF BEEF:

1 whole rib-eye of beef on the bone approx 1kg.
Vegetable oil for frying
1 tablespoon curly parsley, chopped

Season the beef with salt liberally and fry in a heavy-based pan with the vegetable oil until nicely coloured.
Transfer to a pre-heated oven and cook at 200°C (Gas mark 6).
For medium rare cook for 6 minutes on one side, turn the beef over and cook for a further 6 minutes. For well done increase the cooking by another five minutes per side.
Remove to a cooling wire rack and allow meat to rest for 10 minutes before carving.

TO SERVE:

Sauté the artichoke pieces in a little olive oil until golden brown.
Warm the pommes sautées through in a separate pan and then add the artichokes and French beans.
Mix all the vegetables together until warmed through, season with salt and pepper, and arrange them on the centre of a large warm serving plate.
Cut thick slices of the beef and lay them on top.
Sprinkle with the chopped parsley.

A tagine is a type of North African dish which is normally slow cooked at a low temperature making it very tender and aromatic. Generally, tagines are some sort of stew, primarily lamb oriented, though poultry is not uncommon, with a mixture of vegetables, often with the addition of fruit. The fruits are generally used in dried form and create a unique taste - adding a subtle sweetness to the overall flavour. It is common for tagines to contain preserved lemons. Originally tagines were cooked for many hours, although in modern cooking conditions good results can be achieved in about one and a half hours. Still, the longer it is cooked the better and richer the flavours become.

tagine

A tagine is also the special pot to cook these dishes in. The typical tagine pot is made of heavy clay which can be sometimes painted or glazed. It consists of two parts; a base unit which is flat and circular with low sides, and a large cone or dome-shaped cover that sits inside the base during cooking. This dish tastes delicious served with couscous, a small granular type of pasta which is made by sprinkling durum or hard wheat semolina grains with cold salted water and rolling and coating them in fine wheat flour. It's a staple ingredient in North Africa. Traditional couscous can be bought in the UK, but needs pre-soaking and takes a long time to cook - it's usually steamed. The quick-cook couscous is more convenient and involves just soaking or simmering the couscous in boiling water for about ten minutes to rehydrate it.

SERVES 4

TAGINE OF CHICKEN WITH CONFIT LEMON AND BLACK OLIVES

100g root ginger, peeled
1 small white onion, peeled
3 sticks celery
1 teaspoon coriander seeds
2 ripe plum tomatoes
1 medium sized organic / free-range chicken
4 tablespoons extra virgin olive oil
3 cloves garlic, crushed
1 pinch saffron thread
1 teaspoon ground cumin
120g pitted kalamata olives
1 green pepper
Sea salt
Ground white pepper
220ml dry white wine
1 small jar preserved / confit lemons

Finely chop the ginger, onion and celery.
Crush the coriander seeds.
Drop the tomatoes into boiling water for 30 seconds and then into iced water and remove the skin.
Cut them into dice.
Joint the chicken into eight pieces.
Heat the olive oil in a large, heavy casserole pan.
Brown the chicken well on all sides in the pan.
Add the onions to the pan and cook gently for 5 minutes.
Add the garlic, ginger, saffron, celery, cumin, coriander, olives, tomatoes and green pepper.
Season with a pinch of salt and pepper and stir well.
Add the wine and bring to the boil.
Transfer all into a tagine dish and cook with the lid on, in the oven at 200°C (Gas mark 6) for 45 minutes.
Add the lemons and replace the lid.
Turn the oven off and put the tagine back in, with the door open, for 10 minutes.

TO SERVE:

Serve at the table from the tagine dish along with some couscous and salad.

I really like this dish because it's an unusual combination of flavours which work well together. Use a good quality beer, perhaps Belgian or organic, and good quality free-range or organic chicken, as it holds up to this style of slow cooking. This is a great dish; as it slow cooks you can enjoy a glass of wine before dinner and you can serve it straight from the oven to the table.

SERVES 6

2 x 1.5kg whole chickens
50g unsalted butter
2 shallots, peeled and diced
75ml gin
1 bay leaf
1 sprig thyme
600g white button mushrooms, washed and evenly sliced
700ml Belgian beer
250ml double cream
100ml crème fraîche
Salt and pepper
2 tablespoons curly parsley, chopped

First prepare the chicken by removing the legs and separating the thigh and drumsticks.
Cut off the bottom of the carcass leaving the breasts on the bone.
Cut this into 4 even pieces.
Heat some vegetable oil in a large pan and brown the chicken pieces evenly.
Remove the chicken from the pan and set aside.
Pour off the oil from the pan.
Place the butter into the pan with the shallots and cook gently for 2-3 minutes without colouring.
Add the gin to the pan and flambé by igniting the liquid with a lighter when it enters the hot pan.
Place the chicken back in the pan along with the bay leaf, thyme, mushrooms and the beer.
Return the liquid to the boil and then turn it down to a gentle simmer.
After 45 minutes of cooking, remove the chicken.
Add the cream and crème fraîche to the pan, bring it back to the boil and reduce the sauce by one third.
Adjust the seasoning of the sauce with salt and pepper and finish with the chopped parsley.

TO SERVE:
Arrange the chicken pieces on the plates and pour over the sauce and mushrooms.
Sautéed potatoes would be a nice accompaniment to this dish.

CHICKEN COOKED IN BEER

BRAISED SHIN OF BEEF

Cuts of meat that can only be cooked to perfection by slowly braising them in stock with vegetables and aromatics are hugely rewarding to cook with. At the restaurant we prepare a lot of dishes in this way. I think it is a true test of the chef's skills to take a tough cut of meat and end up with it seasoned correctly and the sauce at the right consistency. A few basics are required. Use a good rich red wine such as Cabernet Sauvignon, fresh herbs and vegetables and, most importantly, some home-made stocks. You will also need a good heavy pot, like a Le Creuset, which will retain an even heat while braising in the oven. Beef shin is a particularly good cut as it has a generous amount of gelatinous fibre. This will help stop the meat from drying out when cooking. Ask your local butcher to order some in for you and to cut the shin into large even-sized pieces. Remember, ovens may vary in temperature, so you may have to add more water to the beef while cooking.

SERVES 4-6

2.5kg boneless shin of beef
1 bottle of red wine (Cabernet Sauvignon)
1 medium onion
1 large carrot
3 celery stalks
50g unsalted butter
30g plain flour
3 sprigs fresh thyme
1 head garlic, halved
1½ litres beef stock - *see basic 5*
2 litres chicken stock - *see basic 3*
Vegetable oil for frying

Trim the shin of beef of all silver sinew and cut it into 5cm pieces.
Place it in a large bowl, cover with red wine and leave for 24 hours.

THE NEXT DAY...

COOKING THE BEEF:

Drain the meat and place on a kitchen towel to remove any excess moisture, keeping the wine to use later on.

Season the meat well with salt and colour in vegetable oil in a very hot pan until dark brown on all sides.
Lift the meat out into a suitable casserole pan.
De-glaze the browning pan with a little water and add this to the meat.
Peel and chop the vegetables into 3cm dice.
Melt the butter in the pan and cook the vegetables in the butter until golden brown. Add these to the meat.
Add the red wine to the casserole pan and reduce until it becomes a glaze then add the flour and mix well.
Add the thyme, garlic, beef and chicken stock to the casserole and bring it to the boil then place a paper lid on top and cook in an oven, pre-heated to 180°C (Gas mark 4), for 2½ to 3 hours.
Remove the casserole from the oven, the beef should be very tender so that you can cut it with a spoon and the sauce is rich and dark in colour.
Allow the casserole to cool down before removing the beef and passing the sauce through a fine sieve.

TO SERVE:

Warm the pieces of beef in the sauce and serve in a large dish at the table with some mashed potatoes, and some boiled root vegetables

Spätzle, a welcome change to pasta, pulses and starches…

ROAST LOIN OF VENISON WITH BRAISED SAVOY CABBAGE, SPÄTZLE AND CHICKEN JUS

Spätzle is a form of pasta made with a batter composed of flour, milk, egg, salt and nutmeg. You can master the technique for Spätzle by scraping small amounts off a chopping board into a pan of boiling water. Chop them into irregular shapes and thin pieces. It will cook in a matter of minutes. Before serving it is quickly sautéed in a little butter to crisp its texture. It makes a welcome change to pasta, pulses and starches. The braised cabbage is also great to eat with chicken, pheasant and game.

Venison is a delicious and tender meat that can be prepared as easily as top quality beef, but is much lower in saturated fat and cholesterol. Scottish venison is highly nutritious and rich in protein and is a fabulous alternative to other meats

SERVES 6

6 x 130g portions of venison loin, fully trimmed of sinew
Vegetable oil for frying
Salt

Season each portion with salt and pre-heat oven to 200°C (Gas mark 6).
Warm a sauté pan with 1 tablespoon vegetable oil.
When a good heat rises, caramelise all sides of the venison until light brown.
Place the venison onto a tray and cook in the oven and cook for 6-10 minutes depending on the thickness of the loin.
Allow to rest for 5 minutes before carving

1 quantity of Spätzle mixture - *see basic 14*
Drain the Spätzle once they are all cooked and place in bowl until ready to re-heat.

1 quantity braised Savoy cabbage - *see basic 18*
1 quantity chicken jus - *see basic 8*

TO SERVE:

Place two or three spoonfuls of the cabbage in the centre of each plate.
Warm the Spätzle by sautéeing quickly in a little butter, and place next to the cabbage.
Slice the loin of venison into 5-6 slices and serve with some warm chicken jus.

CONFIT LEG OF CHICKEN WITH MADEIRA, WALNUTS AND FRESH PASTA

Confit is essentially poaching in oil or fat at a low temperature. It is a technique that we frequently use at the restaurant and is a very versatile method of cooking, suitable for meat and fish as well as certain vegetables such as garlic and shallots. The tenderness achieved with confiting the chicken legs, cannot be matched by simply roasting them. It will leave the meat simply falling away from the bone. Making fresh pasta is of course a more time consuming process than buying ready-made pasta, but I feel that it is worthwhile persevering with until you master your own technique. If, however, time in the kitchen is short, buy good quality ready-made pasta. Finish the dish with a creamy Madeira sauce with walnuts. It transforms a humble leg of chicken into something both rich and satisfying.

SERVES 6

CONFIT LEG OF CHICKEN WITH MADEIRA, WALNUTS AND FRESH PASTA

CONFIT CHICKEN LEGS:

6 chicken legs
1kg duck fat

Lightly season the chicken legs and fry them in a heavy-based pan with vegetable oil to take on a light golden colour.
Melt the duck fat in a pan and add the chicken legs to it. The legs should be just covered with the fat.
Bring the fat up to boiling point and then transfer to a low oven, approximately 120°C - 140°C (Gas mark ½-1), to cook for about 1½ hours or until the meat is very tender (the bone should come away from the meat with little effort).
Allow to cool in the fat and then carefully transfer to a tray to drain off the excess fat.

Note: *The duck fat should not boil in the oven. Duck fat can be stored in the fridge and re-used up to 3 or 4 times.*

MADEIRA SAUCE:

375ml Madeira wine
1 shallot
500ml chicken stock - *see basic 3*
500ml double cream

Peel and finely slice the shallot and place it in a pan with the Madeira.
Put the pan on the heat and cook until the Madeira is reduced by half.
Add the chicken stock to the pan and reduce the volume by half again.
Add the double cream, bring to the boil and then remove the sauce from the heat.
Strain the sauce through a fine mesh sieve into a suitable container cover with cling film and set aside.

WALNUTS:

36 shelled walnut halves
Cold milk

Place the walnuts in a pan with enough cold milk to cover them.
Bring the milk to the boil and allow it to simmer for 1 minute.
Remove the pan from the heat and allow it to stand for a further 5 minutes to cool slightly.
Peel the skin from the walnuts with the pointed tip of a small knife to help get into the small gaps.
Set the nuts aside until required. Discard the skin. (The milk can be used to make a custard or ice cream)

TO FINISH AND SERVE:

1 quantity pasta - *see basic 13*
cut into tagliatelle

Place the chicken legs on a tray skin side up under a pre-heated grill to crisp the skin without burning.
Cook the pasta in well salted boiling water and divide between six plates when cooked and drained.
Place the chicken legs on top of the pasta.
Re-heat the sauce with the walnuts in a saucepan and spoon it over the chicken.

Meat and fruit can work really well together and pork and apples are a great traditional partnership. When buying your meat for this dish, ensure you buy a quality piece of pork from a good butcher or your local farmers' market. Breeds that would work well in this recipe would include Tamworth, Gloucester Old Spot or even Wild Boar. Chestnuts are a popular ingredient in French cookery, whereas we more commonly associate them here with Christmas. They can be bought from the supermarket pre-cooked in vacuum-packed bags for ease of use. Aside from the classic combination of pork and apples you can also use pears, plums, or even rhubarb, to accompany the pork.

SERVES 6

6 x 150g portions of pork loin
3 Braeburn apples
100ml rich Madeira (Blandy's Duke of Clarence)
250g cooked sweet chestnuts
400ml fresh chicken stock - *see basic 3*
250g unsalted butter
1 large onion, peeled and finely diced
6 portions curly kale
Salt

Season the pork with salt and fry in a little oil until well coloured on all sides.
Place the pork on a tray and cook in the oven at 220°C (Gas mark 7) for 15-20 minutes until just cooked.
Keep the pan aside unwashed.
Remove the pork from the oven and place in a warm place to rest.
Peel the apples and cut into 1cm thick wedges, removing the core.
Set aside.
Pour the oil from the pan the pork was cooked in and place it back on the heat.
De-glaze the pan with the Madeira.
Add the chestnuts to the pan and cook until the Madeira has reduced by half.
Add the chicken stock and cook on a high heat until it has reduced by half again.
Melt 100g butter, add the apples and cook for 1 minute until the liquid has become a thick glaze.
Melt the remaining 150g butter in a wide, heavy-based pan and cook the onion gently with a pinch of salt for 5 minutes until soft but not coloured.
Tear the kale into 3cm pieces, discarding the tough stalks, and add to the pan with 1 tablespoon of water and a pinch of salt.
Sauté on a medium heat until just cooked.

TO SERVE:

Divide the kale between six plates and slice each portion of pork on top.
Place the apple and chestnut mix onto the plates and drizzle with the pan liquor.

PORK LOIN, SAUTÉED KALE, APPLES AND CHESTNUTS

A good pheasant is extremely tasty - it must be hung for a few days to develop its flavour, so check with your butcher or game dealer how long it has been hung. All game birds need care to prevent them from over-cooking so a nice piece of streaky bacon tied onto the breasts, or some butter applied under the skin, will help to maintain moisture. The younger birds are better for roasting and the hen is generally enough to feed two. Serve with some puy (French) or green lentils along with bacon lardons and salsify, which is a long thin root vegetable and tastes a little like an artichoke. This will make a healthy and tasty winter Sunday dinner.

SERVES 6

ROAST HEN PHEASANTS WITH PUY LENTILS, LARDONS AND SALSIFY

ROAST HEN PHEASANTS WITH PUY LENTILS, LARDONS AND SALSIFY

PHEASANTS:

3 x 750-900g young hen pheasants, plucked
6 slices of streaky unsmoked bacon
4 tablespoons vegetable oil
1 carrot, peeled and chopped
1 onion, peeled and chopped
1 stick celery, chopped
2 cloves garlic, peeled
6 juniper berries, crushed
Salt and pepper

Pre-heat the oven to 200°C (Gas mark 6).
Cover each of the pheasants with 2 slices of the bacon and tie down with some string. Season the inside of the carcass with a couple of pinches of salt.
Heat the vegetable oil in a large roasting tray and when you feel a good heat rising, place the birds in the tray and brown all sides.
Add the carrots, onion, celery, garlic and juniper berries around the birds and place in the oven for 25-30 minutes basting the birds frequently.

LENTILS:

120g Puy lentils (soaked in cold water for one hour)
50g whole piece unsmoked bacon or bone
2 sprigs fresh thyme
2 cloves garlic, peeled
1 small onion, peeled and cut in half
600ml chicken stock - *see basic 3*
4 sticks of salsify
30 bacon lardons, fried until golden

While the birds are roasting, place the pre-soaked lentils in a large pot.
Add the whole bacon, thyme, garlic and onion and pour over the chicken stock.
Bring to the boil and simmer for 25-30 minutes.
When cooked season the lentils with salt and freshly ground pepper.
Remove and discard the thyme sprigs, onion and bacon.
Peel and wash the salsify, cut into 3cm long batons and cook in boiling salted water for 5-10 minutes.
Strain, then sauté until golden brown in a little oil along with the lardons, drain on some kitchen paper and stir into the cooked lentils.

TO FINISH AND SERVE:

350ml chicken stock - *see basic 3*
50g butter

Remove the pheasants from the oven and leave to rest for 10-15 minutes.
Lift the pheasants from the roasting tray and place them in a large serving dish, leaving the vegetables in the tray.
Pour off any excess fat from the roasting tray, return to the stove and add the chicken stock to the vegetables and boil until reduced by half, skimming frequently.
Strain the sauce into a small pan, discard the vegetables and whisk in the butter, place the sauce aside.
Arrange the warm lentils around the pheasant and present them at the table.
Serve by dividing first the legs then the breast.
Spoon some of the lentils and salsify into each plate, place a portion of leg and breast on top, pour over a little of the sauce.
Serve with some seasonal vegetables of your choice.

This recipe gives an alternative way of serving Spätzle, the alternative to pasta or potatoes which originated in southern Germany. It is a simple and quick recipe to prepare. Spätzle are great with either fish or meat, but in this recipe I serve them with sautéed oyster mushrooms, spinach and a light white wine sauce. **SERVES 6**

SPÄTZLE WITH OYSTER MUSHROOMS, BABY SPINACH AND WHITE WINE VELOUTÉ

1 quantity Spätzle - *see basic 14*

1 quantity white wine velouté - *see basic 10*

TO FINISH:

300g oyster mushrooms

200g baby spinach, washed

2 tablespoons parsley, chopped

Salt and freshly ground white pepper

Slice the oyster mushrooms into thin strips and sauté them to a golden colour with a little butter and some salt and freshly ground white pepper.

Cook the spinach in a large pan with a small amount of butter and season with a little salt.

Warm a tablespoon of olive oil in a large non-stick pan and, when hot, carefully sauté a few portions of the Spätzle in the pan until it becomes slightly crisp and golden in colour.

TO SERVE:

Spoon an even amount of spinach onto the centre of each plate and place some oyster mushrooms on top.

Arrange the Spätzle on top of the mushrooms and serve with the warm white wine velouté and a little chopped parsley.

Like hummingbirds lured to nectar, human resolve is wonderfully powerless in the face of a good dessert. What you serve as the pièce de résistance of a meal, from a delectable chilled lime soufflé to decadent steamed pudding, should of course harmonise with what has gone before. Most of the desserts to follow are served in the restaurant and have been developed in collaboration with my pastry chef Rikki Preston. Some pleasures should never be denied.

Desserts

These chilled lime soufflés are similar to a frozen parfait or ice cream. They are a great idea to serve as a dinner party dessert as they are very refreshing and not too heavy. You can of course substitute limes with another intense, sharp fruit like lemons or passion fruit. Remove the soufflés from the freezer 10 minutes before serving them to give them time to soften a little in the centre.

SERVES 6

CHILLED LIME SOUFFLÉ

1 leaf gelatine
255ml double cream
3 limes, juice and zest
4 egg yolks
75g caster sugar
4 egg whites
6 ramekins 6-8cm across

Soak the gelatine in ice cold water for five minutes until soft.
Whip the cream in a bowl until it holds its shape, but is not too stiff.
Add the lime juice and zest and fold carefully into the cream.
Put the egg yolks and half of the sugar into a bowl and whisk until they become pale and aerated. An electric mixer will give the best results.
Put a couple of tablespoons of the cream into a pan and warm gently.
Drain the gelatine of the water and dissolve it in the pan with the cream.
Add this cream to the egg yolks and mix well.
Whip the egg whites with the remaining sugar in a large bowl to form a soft meringue.
Using a spatula or a large whisk fold together the whipped cream and egg yolk mixtures, trying to retain as much air as possible.
Finally fold in the egg whites one third at a time.
Cut strips of silicone paper and wrap around the outsides of the ramekins so that it sticks up above the top of the ramekin by 5cm. Secure with a small piece of sticky tape.
Spoon the mixture into each one and fill to one third over the top of the ramekin.
Place the ramekins in the freezer for 2 hours to set.

TO SERVE:
Remove the paper from the ramekins and leave at room temperature for 5-10 minutes before serving.

Rhubarb can be found in season as early as March, when you can buy the tender pink stalks that have a delicate flavour which is recognised as forced rhubarb. Towards May it starts to turn a deeper, rosier red and becomes more acidic too. This vanilla panna cotta dessert can be served with a variety of different fruit compotes, but rhubarb is a perfect match as its tartness complements the creamy and slightly sweet panna cotta. It's worth spending money on vanilla pods rather than essence for this recipe - there's no substitute for the flavour of the real thing. You can store them in a jar filled with caster sugar as this will help stop them drying out and also infuses the sugar with its aroma so you can use it for other desserts.

SERVES 8

RHUBARB COMPOTE:

225g rhubarb, washed and chopped
60g caster sugar
30ml water
5g diced stem ginger

Put the rhubarb, sugar and water into a saucepan.
Cook on a gentle heat until the sugar has dissolved and the rhubarb is tender.
Add the diced ginger and remove the pan from the heat.
Set aside to infuse and cool.
Put 1 spoonful of this mix into each serving dish (e.g. a cocktail glass or ramekin).
Place in the fridge.

VANILLA PANNA COTTA:

1 vanilla pod
300ml double cream
75ml milk
65g caster sugar
1½ leaves gelatine

Split the vanilla pod in half lengthways and scrape out the seeds into a pan with the milk and cream and sugar.
Place the pan on the stove and slowly bring it up to a simmer.
Soak the gelatine for 5 minutes in ice cold water until soft.
Squeeze out the excess water and whisk to dissolve the gelatine in the cream mixture.
Remove the pan from the heat and allow the cream to cool to body temperature.
Place the mix in the fridge and stir every 5 minutes until thick enough to suspend the vanilla seeds.
Pour the mix over the rhubarb compote in the serving dishes, leaving at least 1cm space at the top.
Return to the fridge to set.

TO SERVE:

Take the panna cotta out of the fridge 15 minutes before serving to let it come up to room temperature.

VANILLA PANNA COTTA WITH RHUBARB AND GINGER COMPOTE

This dish is really light and tasty with citrus fruits through it, perfect for a special occasion or you could use it as a dish between courses to cleanse the palate. If you preferred, you could also substitute the champagne with a still wine. SERVES 12

CHAMPAGNE AND CITRUS TERRINE

10 leaves gelatine
1 bottle of champagne / cava
450g caster sugar
Juice 1 lemon
Juice 1 orange
10 oranges
10 pink grapefruit
28cm terrine mould

Put the gelatine leaves into a bowl of ice cold water for five minutes to soften.
Put the champagne into a saucepan with the sugar, lemon and orange juices, and bring it to the boil, mixing well until all the sugar has dissolved.
Remove the pan from the heat and stir in the softened gelatine to dissolve it and set it aside off the stove to cool to room temperature.
Meanwhile peel the oranges and grapefruits removing the skin and white pith.
Cut the segments from the fruit with a small knife and set aside.
Line a terrine with cling film as smoothly as possible, then pour in 1cm of the jelly and place the terrine in the fridge to set.
Once the jelly has set lift the terrine out of the fridge and place a layer of fruit segments running in line with the terrine.
Cover the layer of segments with more of the jelly and return to the fridge to set once again.
Repeat the process until the terrine is full; you should finish with a layer of the jelly. If the jelly starts to set at room temperature in the pan you can melt it back by heating it gently again on the stove.
Place the terrine in the fridge to set completely before use.

TO SERVE:

Lift the terrine out of the mould and unwrap it from the cling film.
Cut the terrine with a hot knife into slices approximately 1.5 to 2cm thick.
Place the slices of terrine lying flat on the serving plates.
Garnish with a little finely sliced mint or a passionfruit coulis.

Eating delicious peaches ripe and fragrant, freshly fallen from the trees in the Mediterranean is something I highly recommend if it is something that you have never experienced. When we are lucky enough to eat them like that, ready, ripe and warm from the sun, the flavours speak for themselves. Both nectarines and peaches come with white flesh, but the yellow, in my opinion, has more flavour. However, unripe peaches and nectarines can be somewhat improved by cooking, so poaching them is a good idea. In this recipe the poached peach is set off by rosemary cream. The ancient Greeks said that rosemary was good for the brain, a theory that has persisted throughout the centuries. Be that as it may, the Italians love its strong spicy flavour, whilst the French use it more subtly. Rosemary is a most versatile herb with a flavour that complements a wide variety of dishes and ingredients. Native to the Mediterranean, its bittersweet green leaves look similar to pine needles. The plant is an evergreen shrub, and grows easily into a sturdy bush, so the leaves are available fresh all year round. When used sparingly, the flavour of rosemary goes well in subtle and delicate dishes such as ice creams, sorbets, fools and fruit salads.

SERVES 6

POACHED PEACHES WITH ROSEMARY CREAM

POACHED PEACHES:

3 nice ripe peaches

1 litre water

500g caster sugar

Cut the peaches in half and remove the stone.

Put the water and sugar into a deep saucepan and bring it to the boil.

Add the peaches to the pan and cover with a round sheet of greaseproof paper.

Turn down to a low heat and leave to simmer until the skin of the peaches can be easily removed.

Remove the pan from the heat and leave to cool.

ROSEMARY CREAM:

2 leaves gelatine

6 sprigs fresh rosemary

350ml double cream

60g caster sugar

Put the gelatine leaves in ice cold water for five minutes until soft.

Pull the rosemary leaves off the stalks and discard the stalks.

Place the cream and sugar in a heavy-based saucepan and bring it to the boil, then add the rosemary leaves.

Add the softened gelatine leaves to the pan and stir to dissolve them.

Remove the pan from the heat and leave the mix to cool and infuse.

Once cooled slightly, strain the cream through a sieve and discard the rosemary leaves.

Pour the mixture evenly into six dariole moulds and place them in the fridge to set for at least one hour.

TO SERVE:

Dip the dariole moulds into a pan of hot water for 3 seconds then turn them upside down to remove the set creams.

Place one cream in the centre of a plate.

Slice the poached peaches evenly and fan one half peach around each cream evenly.

CHOCOLATE PUDDING WITH CRÈME CHANTILLY AND ALMOND ANGLAISE SAUCE

CHOCOLATE PUDDING WITH CRÈME CHANTILLY AND ALMOND ANGLAISE SAUCE

This dish is straightforward to make and consists of ingredients such as cocoa powder, caster sugar and plain flour which most of us have in our kitchen cupboards at home. The almond sauce is a recipe for fresh custard which you will be able to make ahead of time, and can also be served to accompany an array of puddings. The ideal mould to use is aluminium (6cm in diameter and 5cm in height) and should be well buttered inside.

SERVES 4

CHOCOLATE PUDDING:

125g unsalted butter, at room temperature
125g caster sugar
2 eggs
90g plain flour
35g cocoa powder
6g baking powder
2 tablespoons water

Place the butter into the bowl of a food mixer and beat it until it is light and fluffy.
Add the sugar to the butter and continue mixing until the sugar is fully incorporated.
Add the eggs to the mix one at a time while beating.
When all of the eggs are added, beat for a further 4-5 minutes.
Sift the flour, baking powder and cocoa powder together and fold them into the butter mix.
Continue beating the mix until it becomes light and creamy.
Add enough cold water for the mix to reach dropping consistency.
Lightly butter and flour small dariole moulds and pipe in the mix until half full.
Place the moulds on a tray and cook in the oven at 180°C (Gas mark 4) for 8 to 10 minutes.

1 quantity Crème Chantilly - *see basic 27*

1 quantity almond Anglaise sauce - *see basic 28*

TO SERVE:

Pour a little of the warm almond sauce into the bottom of a bowl.
Turn the chocolate pudding upside down and remove it from the mould.
Place the pudding on top of the sauce then spoon the crème Chantilly over the chocolate pudding to serve.

RASPBERRY TRIFLE WITH LIME YOGHURT

This is a variation of a classic British dessert. You can of course use pre-made jelly, but, if you choose to use fresh or frozen whole raspberries, the flavour will be so much better and not be full of preservatives and artificial flavourings.

SERVES 6

RASPBERRY JELLY:

500g frozen raspberries
180g icing sugar
5 leaves gelatine
Juice ½ lemon

Put the raspberries and sugar into a large pan and bring slowly to the boil, stirring occasionally.
Remove the pan from the heat and transfer the contents to a food processor and blend until smooth.
Strain the sauce through a fine sieve into a container and set aside.
Soak the gelatine in ice cold water for five minutes until soft.
Drain the gelatine from the water and add it to a pan with 250ml of the raspberry sauce.
Gently heat the pan to dissolve the gelatine and mix in another 250ml of the sauce off the heat.
Add the lemon juice, mix well and set aside to cool a little.

LIME YOGHURT:

300g full fat Greek yoghurt
1 lime, juice and grated zest
50g icing sugar

Put all of the ingredients together in a bowl and whisk together gently until smooth.

CUSTARD LAYER:

300ml thick custard
200ml double cream

Put the cream into a large bowl and whisk to a ribbon stage.
Add the custard and continue whisking together until the cream thickens.

TO FINISH AND SERVE:

30 fresh raspberries
12 sponge fingers

Break up some sponge fingers and place into the bottom of a cocktail glass.
Add 4-5 raspberries to the glass and pour the jelly in until it covers the raspberries.
Place in the fridge to set firm.
Once the jelly has set, remove it from the fridge and spoon in the custard, filling it to half way up the glass.
Gently add the lime yoghurt to cover the custard and return to the fridge for at least 20 minutes before serving.
Garnish the top of the trifle with some raspberries and some sponge fingers.

vodka and salt

White chocolate is not exactly a true chocolate; it is made from milk, sugar and fat with a little cocoa butter added. You can describe it as having a rather bland and over-sweet taste and is therefore best used to flavour desserts with. At the restaurant we use it to make a lovely hot soufflé or, as in this recipe, it is used to make a delicious light chocolate mousse. You can try adding a few grains of salt, tasting as you go, to see how this actually develops the flavour of the mousse or a few drops of vodka, this works really well too and enhances the taste of the chocolate. Mandarin segments which have been lightly poached in a Cointreau-flavoured syrup accompany the mousse and it is served in a crisp sweet pastry tartlet. In the picture shown I have used a special dome-shaped mould but you can use a piping bag and fluted nozzle to fill the pastry tartlet which will give you just as good an end presentation.

TART OF WHITE CHOCOLATE MOUSSE WITH POACHED MANDARINS

SERVES 6

WHITE CHOCOLATE MOUSSE:

200g white chocolate
2 leaves gelatine
½ pint double cream
2 eggs, separated
Pinch sugar
Pinch salt
6 x 6-8cm stainless steel dome moulds

Melt the chocolate in a bowl over a pan of simmering water.
Soften the gelatine in 50ml of the cream for five minutes and add to the melted chocolate.
In a separate bowl lightly whip the remaining cream.
Remove the bowl from the heat and add the egg yolks, salt and sugar, working it quickly into the chocolate.
Quickly whisk in the whipped cream trying to retain as much air as possible in the mix.
Whip the egg whites in another bowl until you have stiff peaks.
Fold this into the chocolate base one third at a time, making sure the egg whites are evenly mixed through.
Pipe into moulds and place in the fridge to set.

1 quantity sweet pastry - *see basic 26*
6 x 10cm non-stick tartlet moulds

Roll the dough out to about 3mm thickness on a floured surface and line tartlet moulds which have been greased and floured.
Rest the tartlets in the fridge for 30 minutes.
Fill the tartlets with baking beans and cook in the oven at 180°C (Gas mark 4) for 20 minutes, or until the pastry is cooked through.
Remove the beans, turn out the tartlet cases and allow them to cool on a wire rack.

SYRUP FOR POACHED MANDARINS:

100g sugar
50ml water
50ml Cointreau

Boil the sugar, Cointreau and water together in a pan until the sugar has dissolved.
Segment the mandarins and place them in a bowl.
Pour the hot syrup over the segments and leave to cool.

TO SERVE:

Sit the base of the chocolate mousse moulds in boiling water for 3 seconds and turn them upside down into the cooked tartlet cases.
Arrange the mandarin segments around the mousse as desired and finish with a sprig of mint or julienned mint leaves.

TART OF WHITE CHOCOLATE MOUSSE WITH POACHED MANDARINS

TROPICAL FRUIT SALAD, ORANGE JELLY AND CARDAMOM AND MINT INFUSION

This extremely refreshing and light dessert has mouth-watering flavours from the pineapple, mango and watermelon, which are set together in a light orange jelly. Or, if you prefer, cut the fruits and serve separately under the orange jelly. The dish is finished with a simple infusion of fresh mint leaves and three distinctive spices; star anise, clove and cardamom, which work in harmony together producing a brilliant contrast to the fruits, making this a fruit salad with a real difference. When serving at the table, strain the mint infusion through a tea strainer over the jelly

SERVES 6

MINT INFUSION:

8 large mint leaves
3 cardamom pods, lightly crushed
½ star anise
1 clove
300ml water
75g caster sugar

Place the mint, cardamom, star anise and clove in a bowl.
Place the sugar and water into a pan and heat until the sugar has dissolved.
Pour the sugar syrup into the bowl with the spices and allow it to cool and infuse for around 6 hours before use.
Strain the infusion through a fine sieve before serving.

ORANGE JELLY:

250ml freshly squeezed orange juice
90g caster sugar
3 leaves gelatine

Soak the gelatine in ice cold water for five minutes until soft.
Put the orange juice into a pan and heat to around 70°C.
Squeeze the gelatine of any excess water and stir into the orange juice until dissolved.
Keep warm (at room temperature) until required.

PREPARING THE FRUIT:

1 golden pineapple
½ small watermelon
2 medium ripe mangos

Cut away the top and bottom of the pineapple and remove the skin.
Cut the pineapple into quarters and remove the core.
Chop the pineapple flesh into small 5mm dice and prepare the mango and the watermelon the same way.
Mix the fruit together in a bowl.
Fill 6 medium-sized ramekins with the chopped fruit and pour the jelly over until it reaches the top and place them in the fridge for 2 hours to set firm.

TO SERVE:

Dip the ramekins in hot water for a few seconds and then pull the jelly gently away from the sides.
Invert the moulds and gently shake out the jellies onto individual soup plates.
Serve with a small ladle of the strained cardamom infusion.

STRAWBERRY MOUSSE WITH LEMON GRASS JELLY AND RHUBARB GRANITÉ

This is a beautifully fresh dessert for warm summer days. The three distinct flavours work in harmony without overpowering each other. I would always recommend buying Scottish strawberries, particularly the sweet Jubilee variety which is readily available in many shops and supermarkets. The rhubarb granité is a slowly frozen flavoured sugar syrup which consists of ice crystals (up to 3mm long) which are crushed with a fork to create a slush texture.

This dessert is best served in a glass, finished with rhubarb granité served at the table. SERVES 6

STRAWBERRY MOUSSE WITH LEMON GRASS JELLY AND RHUBARB GRANITÉ

STRAWBERRY MOUSSE:

500g fresh strawberries
150g icing sugar
4 leaves gelatine
1 teaspoon lemon juice

Wash the strawberries and remove the tops.
Cut them in half and place in a bowl with the sugar.
Set aside for 1 hour to let the sugar draw out the juices from the strawberries.
Place the contents of the bowl into a food processor and blend to a purée.
Strain the purée through a fine sieve and discard the seeds.
Soak the gelatine in ice cold water for five minutes until it softens.
Gently warm the strawberry juice and add the gelatine, stirring until it has dissolved.
Taste the purée and check for sweetness, dissolving a little extra sugar into the hot purée if required.
Add the lemon juice.
Fill a large glass to one third of its volume with the purée and place it in the fridge for at least an hour to set.

RHUBARB GRANITÉ:

110g pink rhubarb
40g caster sugar
80ml water
Lemon juice
Fresh white peppercorns in a pepper mill

Wash and finely slice the rhubarb and place it into a pan with the water.
Add the sugar and lemon juice, bring it to the boil and allow it to simmer for 2 minutes until soft.
Place the contents of the pan into a liquidiser with 4-6 turns of the white pepper and blend until smooth.
Strain the purée through a fine sieve and transfer into a shallow tray.
Place the tray into the freezer and mix the granité with a fork every 20 minutes until it is firm but not solid.

LEMON GRASS JELLY:

4 sticks lemon grass
2 leaves gelatine
75g sugar
300ml water
1 chamomile tea bag

Split the lemon grass sticks in half lengthways with a knife.
Soak the gelatine in ice cold water for five minutes until soft.
Put the sugar, water and lemon grass into a pan and bring to the boil until the sugar is dissolved.
Remove the pan from the heat and stir in the gelatine leaves until dissolved.
Add the tea bag to the pan and allow it to infuse until the liquid has cooled.
Remove the bag and strain the liquid through a sieve into a container and set aside in the fridge.

Note: *This jelly should be slightly runny when serving.*

TO SERVE:

Remove the glasses with the strawberry mousse from the fridge.
Pour over the lemon grass jelly.
With a fork scrape the rhubarb granité until it has completely broken up and looks similar to snow.
Spoon on top of the jellies and serve.

CHOCOLATE SOUP WITH CHERRIES, BLANCHED ALMONDS AND VANILLA CAPPUCCINO

This dessert is certainly one of the favourites at the restaurant during the summer when I am able to buy Morello cherries. They have a wonderful and quite unique concentrated cherry flavour and are best served warm. The warm chocolate soup has a creamy, velvety texture which is delicious with the cherries - think of it as a liquid Black Forest gateau! The fresh almonds in this recipe are sweet and soft with a light crunch. You can buy quality fresh almonds at fruit and vegetable counters of good delis.

Use a good quality dark chocolate, which should have approx 64% cocoa content to make the soup. SERVES 6

90ml full fat milk
260ml double cream
125g dark chocolate, broken into small pieces
30 fresh cherries
1 tablespoon icing sugar
1 lemon
15g and 1 teaspoon caster sugar
½ vanilla pod
5g unsalted butter
40g whole almonds, blanched and peeled

Put 60ml of the milk, 1 teaspoon caster sugar and 180ml of the cream into a pan and bring to the boil.
Remove from the heat and whisk in the chocolate until completely melted.
Cover with cling film and set aside at room temperature.
Cut the cherries in half and remove the stones.
Place the cherry halves in a bowl and dust with a light coating of icing sugar and a few drops of lemon juice.

VANILLA CAPPUCCINO:
Scrape the seeds from the vanilla pod and put in a pan with the remaining milk and cream, the caster sugar and butter.
Warm the vanilla milk to 75°C and remove from the heat.

TO SERVE:
Place an even amount of cherries in the centre of a warm soup plate.
Chop the almonds and sprinkle them on top of the cherries.
Re-heat the chocolate soup to just below a simmer and pour it into the bowl.
Using a hand blender or whisk, whizz the vanilla cappuccino so the air mixes into it and creates a froth.
Gently remove the froth from the surface and spoon over the top of the soup.

I love steamed puddings! Although they tend to be rich and quite heavy, they are a very satisfying way to end a meal. The lemon Anglaise does enhance the ginger flavour but a scoop of good crème fraîche will work just as well.

SERVES 8

GINGER PUDDING:

Golden syrup
65g stem ginger, peeled and sliced
140ml milk
50g plain flour
50g shredded suet
50g fresh breadcrumbs
1 teaspoon ground ginger
1 teaspoon mixed spice
1 teaspoon baking powder
1 teaspoon bicarbonate of soda
1 small egg

Grease 8 pudding moulds with softened butter and coat lightly with flour, tipping out the excess.
Pour about 1 tablespoon of golden syrup into each mould.
Place the stem ginger and the milk into a saucepan and bring it to the boil, then remove it from the heat.
Allow it to cool and then strain it through a fine sieve.
Sift all of the dry ingredients into a large mixing bowl and mix well.
Mix in the cooled milk and then beat in the egg until well combined.
Pour the mixture into the prepared moulds until half full and cover each mould with foil.
Place the puddings into a deep oven tray.
Fill the tray with hot water until it reaches half way up the pudding moulds.
Put the tray into a pre-heated oven at 180°C (Gas mark 4) for 35-45 minutes until they are firm to the touch and cooked through (alternatively test with a skewer, it should come out clean).
Remove the puddings from the moulds while hot and serve immediately.

SERVE WITH:

1 quantity lemon Anglaise sauce - *see basic 29*

Note: *You can serve the Anglaise warm or cold, but do not allow it to boil as the eggs will scramble.*

STEAMED GINGER PUDDING WITH LEMON ANGLAISE SAUCE

This is a delicious summer pudding which is full of summer flavours and has a tropical aroma. Be careful when preparing the mango not to get any on your clothes as it stains terribly.

You can use good quality ready-made meringues, but I would recommend making your own. Serve in a tall glass to show off the bright colours. It is best eaten within an hour, so the meringue stays crisp. SERVES 8

MANGO CHANTILLY WITH CRUSHED MERINGUE AND STRAWBERRY SAUCE

MANGO CHANTILLY:

2 ripe mangos

750ml double cream

80g icing sugar

4 ready-made meringues, crushed

Peel the mangos and remove the flesh from the stone using a small knife.

Take one mango and place it in a food processor and blend until smooth. Set aside.

Dice the second mango into small pieces.

Put the double cream and icing sugar in a mixing bowl and whisk to a ribbon stage.

Add the mango coulis to the cream and continue whisking until firm, then fold in the diced mango.

Spoon carefully into a piping bag with a plain wide nozzle.

STRAWBERRY SAUCE:

1 punnet strawberries

80g icing sugar

1 tablespoon fresh lemon juice

Remove the stem from the strawberries.

Wash the fruit in cold water and pat them dry with a paper towel.

Place the strawberries and the icing sugar into a food processor and blend until smooth.

Strain the sauce through a fine sieve.

Finish with the lemon juice to taste.

TO FINISH AND SERVE:

Fill each glass with a little of the mango mix, then add a couple of tablespoons of strawberry sauce and some of the crushed meringue.

Repeat the process until the glass is almost full.

Place the glasses in the fridge until you are ready to serve.

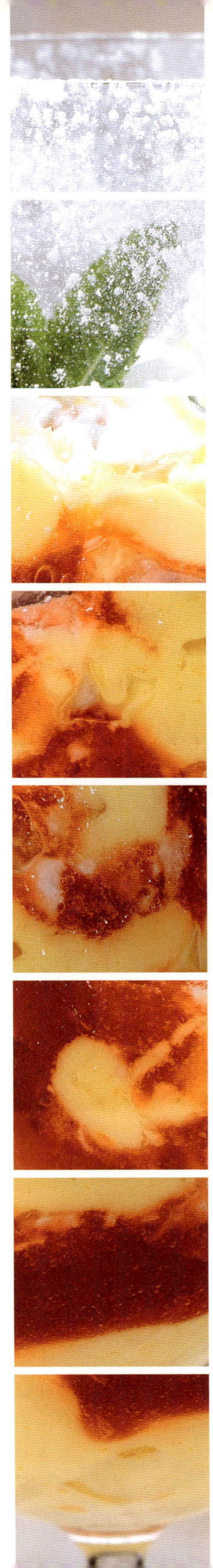

APRICOT AND ALMOND TART WITH CRÈME FRAÎCHE

This is a classic dessert and is an all-time favourite of mine. I just find the sweetness of the almond filling and the slight tartness of the apricots is perfect as a dinner dessert. It's also great in the afternoon with a cup of tea. It is something that you can prepare in advance and will keep for a couple of days.

SERVES 8

SWEET PASTRY:

1 quantity of sweet pastry - *see basic 26*

FRANGIPANE:

125g butter
125g icing sugar
125g ground almonds
25g plain flour
4 eggs

Cut the butter into dice and soften to room temperature.
Sieve the icing sugar into a bowl and add the butter.
Beat together until white and creamy.
Fold in the ground almonds and flour.
Beat the eggs into the mix one at a time until incorporated well.

Note: *For the best results beat the frangipane for 3 minutes to give a lighter texture.*

COOKING AND SERVING:

10 whole apricots
Small tub of crème fraîche
Sprig fresh mint

Pre-heat the oven to 190°C (Gas mark 5).
Butter and flour a 30cm flan ring.
Roll out the sweet pastry to 5mm thickness and place into the flan ring, pressing it into the corners.
Prick the base with a fork.
Spoon the frangipane mixture into the flan and spread it out evenly with a palette knife.
Cut the apricots in half and arrange them on top of the frangipane.
Place the tart in the middle of the oven and bake for 20-25 minutes.
Remove the tart from the oven and allow it to cool for 10 minutes before removing the flan ring.
Serve with a spoon of crème fraîche and a sprig of mint.

I would recommend buying the ripest, softest peaches available. White flesh peaches are perfect for this dish. Ideally it is best to use these fruits at room temperature rather than directly from the fridge.

Sabayon is the French corruption of the Italian word 'zabaglione' and is composed of egg yolks, sugar and wine with the addition of flavourings. It is whisked vigorously in a bowl over a pan of boiling water until it thickens. The combination of heat, speed and air will ensure you are left with a very light mousse that captures the maximum flavour. This can also be used with other seasonal fruits such as berries, apricots and some poached fruits

SERVES 6

GRATIN OF PEACH WITH A KIRSCH SABAYON

KIRSCH CREAM:

4 egg yolks
120g sugar
25g cornflour
600ml milk
300ml whipping cream
2 tablespoons Kirsch

In a bowl, cream the yolks with the sugar until pale in colour.
Add the cornflour, and mix. Bring the milk and cream to the boil.
Pour a little milk over the yolk mixture and mix until smooth.
Add the remaining milk and mix together.
Place the mixture into a saucepan and cook gently until it thickens.
Remove from the heat.
Add the Kirsch, place in a container and leave to cool.

SABAYON:

3 egg yolks
60g sugar
75ml water
20ml Kirsch

Whisk the egg yolks and sugar together in a bowl until pale in colour, then add the water and Kirsch. Whisk together.
Place the bowl over a pan of simmering water.
Continue whisking until the mix doubles in volume.
Remove from the heat.

PREPARE THE FRUIT:

6 ripe peaches - the ripest you can buy

Halve the peaches.
Remove stone then cut each half into four segments.

TO SERVE:

Take six small bowls and arrange the peach segments around the bowl.
Pour over the custard, then top with the sabayon.
Glaze under the grill or use a blowtorch.
Garnish with a sprig of mint.
Vanilla ice cream or sorbet can be served on the side.

satisfaction

CHOCOLATE PAVÉ

If you are a fan of chocolate, then this recipe will definitely satisfy your cravings! First, ensure you buy good quality dark chocolate. I would suggest buying Valrhona or Green & Black's dark chocolate organic range. These are both widely available. Once the chocolate has been melted, a little shot of coffee and a couple of spoonfuls of honey are added to the chocolate along with the whipped cream. I like to use a good Mexican honey as it has a really rich flavour. Before the mixture is added to the terrine mould or cake tin, it is best to line the inside with greaseproof paper, which aids in the removal. Cut it so it sits neatly inside the mould or tin, hanging slightly over the edge. Brushing between the paper and the mould with melted butter will help keep the paper in place when pouring in the mixture. Use a warm, dry carving knife to cut, serving with some warm berries or chopped pistachio nuts.

SERVES 8

guaranteed

CHOCOLATE PAVÉ

70g dark chocolate
130g unsalted butter
125g caster sugar
50g honey
1 shot of espresso
80g cocoa powder
6 egg yolks
225ml double cream

Melt the chocolate in a bowl over a pan of hot water.
Place the butter and the sugar into the bowl of a food mixer and beat until pale and fluffy.
Add the honey, espresso, cocoa powder and egg yolks and continue to beat for 5 minutes until well mixed.
Whisk the cream in a separate bowl until it reaches a ribbon stage (semi-whipped).
Remove the chocolate from the heat and whisk in the lightly whipped cream.
Quickly fold the chocolate cream into the butter mix until it is evenly mixed but still light and fluffy.
Pour the mixture into a terrine mould or cake tin and place in the fridge for about 4 hours until set firm.

TO SERVE:

Use a blowtorch or dip the terrine in hot water to remove the dessert from the mould.
Slice into desired portions using a hot knife and serve on cold plates with some whipped cream and fresh mint.

COFFEE CRÈME BRULÉE

You can use any size of ramekin dish for this recipe, but you may have to adjust the cooking time accordingly. Freshly crushed coffee beans will give the best results, or you can replace the beans with other ingredients or flavourings such as fresh thyme or lavender, which you should infuse in the warm mixture before passing through a sieve and cooking.

SERVES 6

375ml double cream
125ml milk
25g crushed coffee beans
5 egg yolks
100g caster sugar

Bring the milk, cream and crushed coffee beans to the boil in a pan.
In a large bowl whisk together the egg yolks and caster sugar, until a pale yellow colour.
Add the milk and leave to cool for 30 minutes.
Pass the mixture through a sieve and discard the coffee beans.
Pour the mixture into 12 small ramekins approximately 7cm x 3cm deep.
Place in a deep tray filled with boiling water.
Cook in a pre-heated oven 170°C (Gas mark 3) for 20-25 minutes or until the brulées are set.
Chill in the fridge until ready to serve.

Note: *If the brulées start to bubble around the surface, open the door of the oven and turn the temperature down a little.*

TO SERVE:

Remember to remove the brulées from the fridge 30 minutes before serving.
Lightly sprinkle a layer of caster sugar on top and gently caramelise the sugar with a blowtorch or place under a hot grill.
Serve immediately.

PASSION FRUIT SOUP, GRAPEFRUIT AND ORANGE SALAD AND MINT GRANITÉ

This chilled dessert soup has the intense, distinct flavour of passion fruit, balanced by melon. A granité is simply a flavoured water ice and makes a great substitute for sorbet or ice creams - it's like eating freshly fallen snow! The strength of flavour will depend on the amount of mint used and how much time it has had to infuse. Regular mixing during the freezing process is important, and using a fork to scrape the granité into shards will enhance the presentation. In the picture I have served it with some fine slices of orange which have been dipped in a sugar syrup and then dried in an oven at a very low temperature overnight.

SERVES 6

SOUP:

1 ripe Cantaloupe melon
10 whole passion fruits
100ml fresh orange juice
180g icing sugar

Peel the melon and cut it in half.
Remove and discard the seeds, roughly chop the flesh and place it into a liquidiser.
Cut the passion fruits in half and scoop out the seeds and pulp.
Add this to the melon in the liquidiser along with the orange juice and icing sugar.
Blend the ingredients together for one minute until smooth.
Strain the mixture through a fine sieve, pressing as much through as possible with the aid of a ladle and discarding the pulp.
Chill the soup in the fridge until ready to serve.

MINT GRANITÉ:

500ml water
75g caster sugar
8 stems fresh mint

Put the sugar and water into a saucepan and heat it until the sugar has dissolved.
Remove the pan from the heat and add the mint, reserving 6 leaves for the garnish.
Leave to infuse for 15 minutes, then strain the syrup through a fine sieve into a metal or glass tray and place in the freezer.
Return to the mixture every 20 minutes, mixing it with a fork, until it has set firm.
Scrape the surface with the prongs of the fork to form a powder or slush.
This should be done a few hours before you intend to serve the dessert.

PASSION FRUIT SOUP, GRAPEFRUIT AND ORANGE SALAD AND MINT GRANITÉ

TO FINISH AND SERVE:

2 whole passion fruit
3 oranges
1 pink grapefruit

Remove the tops and bottoms of the oranges and grapefruit using a small sharp knife.
Remove the skin and the white pith from the fruit and then cut out the segments and dice them.
Cut the two passion fruits in half and scoop out the flesh and seeds.
Mix the passion fruits with the fruit segments and place a spoonful into each chilled serving dish.
Pour a portion of the chilled soup over the segments and serve.
When at the table, spoon the mint granité into the centre of each bowl and finish with a mint leaf.

RED BERRY SOUP WITH MANGO

I like the idea of cold, chilled berry soup - it's light and refreshing to eat and simple to prepare. It can be made with or without the cava. I would recommend using 3 Pakistan mangos, they are longer, narrower and a paler yellow colour with a sweeter flavour. Failing that, any mangos from South America are delicious, although these are larger so you will only require 2 mango fruits for this recipe.

SERVES 6

500g frozen mixed berries (raspberries, strawberries, blueberries etc…)
90g caster sugar
80ml water
Juice 1 lemon
2-3 mangos
6 mint leaves
100g fresh raspberries
100g fresh blueberries
Icing sugar
150ml cava sparkling wine

Place the frozen berries in a large glass or stainless steel bowl along with the sugar and water, then cover tightly with cling film and set aside.
Bring a large pan of water to the boil then turn it down to a simmer and place the bowl of frozen berries on top.

Note: *Three-quarters of the bowl should be sitting inside the pan.*

Leave the berries to lightly steam away for 45-60 minutes so their juices are extracted.
Remove the bowl from the pan and strain the berry juices through a sieve or hang in a large piece of muslin cloth to allow all the juices to drip through. This will take a couple of hours.
Discard the solids that are left or they can be used elsewhere.
Check the flavour of the soup and, if required, add a few drops of lemon juice.
Chill in the fridge before serving.

TO SERVE:
Peel and cut the mango into small dice.
Finely slice the mint leaves and place them in a bowl with the mango, fresh berries and a dusting of icing sugar and mix gently but thoroughly.
Serve the mixed berries in the centre of a soup bowl pouring the chilled red berry soup over the top.
To finish, pour some of the chilled cava into the soup at the table.

BILLECART-SALMON

An accomplished artist or sportsman has an excellent grasp of basic skills at the heart of his or her work. So too has a great cook. Master the foundations of flavour - the sauces, stocks and vegetable garnishes for which the best quality ingredients should be sought. Acquaint yourself with the basics and your cooking instinctively acquires new, interesting depths. And do make life easier by preparing batches of your basics for the freezer, where they're on standby for crucial roles in a diverse range of dishes.

Basics

basic 1.

LOBSTER OR LANGOUSTINE STOCK

1kg langoustine or lobster heads
100ml olive oil
50g unsalted butter
1 onion, peeled and cut into 2cm dice
2 carrots, peeled and cut into 2cm dice
3 sticks celery, cut into 2cm dice
3 star anise
1 teaspoon fennel seeds
1 teaspoon coriander seeds
200ml white wine
2 litres fish stock - *see basic 2*
2 tomatoes
1 bulb garlic

Heat the olive oil in a heavy-based pan on a high heat until almost smoking.
Add the langoustine heads and sauté for 4-5 minutes until they start to caramelise golden brown.
Remove the pan from the heat, place the langoustine heads into a colander and put to one side.
Return the pan to the heat, add the butter and the chopped vegetables and sauté for 3-4 minutes.
Add the star anise, fennel seeds and coriander seeds to the pan.
Pour in the white wine and reduce this to a glaze.
Put the langoustine heads back into the pot and crush them with a rolling pin.
Add the fish stock, tomatoes and garlic cut in half.
Allow this to boil for 30-45 minutes or until the liquid has reduced by two thirds.
Remove from the heat and allow the stock to rest for 1 hour before passing through a fine sieve.
Discard the langoustine heads and chill the stock, or freeze until ready to use.
This stock will keep for 3 days or can be frozen for up to 12 weeks.

basic 2.

FISH STOCK

It is best to use bones or heads from white fish e.g. cod, turbot, hake, monkfish, halibut. If using the heads, remove the gills and eyes first. Avoid oily fish like salmon and mackerel.

2kg white fish bones or heads
50g butter
1 leek, white part only, finely sliced
1 clove garlic, finely sliced
1 small onion, finely sliced
200ml white wine
1 bay leaf
1 small handful fresh parsley

Melt the butter in a large pot, add the vegetables and gently sweat for 2 minutes without colouring them.
Add the white wine and reduce by two thirds, place the bones in the pan, add the bay leaf and parsley and cover with three litres of cold water.
Bring to the boil and lower the heat to a simmer. Skim the stock every 2-3 minutes to remove the scum on the surface as this will help keep the stock clear.
Cook for 25 minutes and then remove the pan from the heat.
Allow to cool and the solids to settle. Slowly pass through a fine mesh sieve.
Chill in the fridge.
This stock will keep for 3 days or can be frozen for up to 12 weeks.

basic 3.
CHICKEN STOCK
(makes 3 litres of stock)

3kg chicken bones or wings
2 carrots, peeled
1 onion, peeled
2 sticks celery, washed
2 sprigs fresh thyme
4 cloves garlic
1 bay leaf
10 white peppercorns
1 tablespoon sea salt

Put the chicken bones in a large pot and cover with 5 litres of cold water.
Bring to the boil, then skim off any scum that rises to the surface.
After 5 minutes add the remaining ingredients, boil for 5 minutes, then reduce the heat to a simmer and cook for 3 hours.
Pass the stock through a fine mesh sieve, then through a piece of muslin cloth to remove all the impurities.
Cool and chill. This can be kept in the fridge for up to 3 days or frozen for up to 12 weeks.

basic 4.
VEAL STOCK

5kg veal knuckle bones
2 pig's trotters, chopped into 3 pieces
3 large onions, cut into large pieces
3 large carrots, cut into large pieces
4 sticks celery, cut into 4 pieces
2 tablespoons tomato purée
750ml red wine
Small bunch fresh thyme

Note: *The pig's trotters will help give some body to the stock when it is cooked.*

Roast the bones and trotters in a hot oven, 200°C (Gas mark 6), turning them occasionally until brown all over.
Then place them in a deep pot and cover by 30cm with cold water.
Pour off the roasting fat from the tray, then add the vegetables and roast until golden brown.
Stir in the tomato purée, add the red wine and transfer to a saucepan.
Reduce the red wine by two thirds, then transfer the vegetables into the large pan with the bones.
Add the thyme, bring to the boil and skim of any scum that rises to the surface.
Simmer for 6 hours, skimming frequently, strain and chill.
This can be kept for up to 5 days in the fridge or frozen for up to 4 months.

basic 5.

BEEF STOCK

3kg beef bones, chopped
2 pig's trotters, chopped into 3 pieces
2 large onions, cut into large pieces
2 large carrots, cut into large pieces
2 sticks celery, cut into 4
1 teaspoon tomato purée
400ml red wine
Small bunch fresh thyme

Note: *Ask your butcher to chop the beef bones into 5cm cubes and the pig's trotters into 3 pieces. The trotters will help give some body to the stock when it is cooked.*

Roast the bones and trotters in a hot oven, 200°C (Gas mark 6), turning them occasionally until brown all over.
Then place them in a deep pot and cover by 20cm with cold water.
Pour off the roasting fat from the bones, then add the vegetables to the tray and roast until golden brown.
Stir in the tomato purée, add the red wine and transfer to a saucepan.
Reduce the red wine with the vegetables by half, then transfer to the beef stock pot.
Add the thyme, bring to the boil and skim of any scum that rises to the surface.
Simmer for 2½ hours, skimming frequently, strain and chill.
This can be kept for up to 5 days in the fridge or frozen for up to 4 months.

basic 6.

VEGETABLE STOCK (NAGE)

500ml cold water
250g onion
250g carrots
250g celery
3 cloves garlic
1 whole star anise
10 white peppercorns
10 coriander seeds
15 fennel seeds
100ml white wine
Small bunch fresh chervil

Wash and peel all the vegetables and cut into evenly sized 1cm dice.
Place them in a large pot and cover with the 500ml of cold water.
Add the spices, then bring the pan to the boil and cook for 10 minutes.
Pour in the wine, add the chervil and boil for a further 2 minutes, then remove the pan from the heat and set aside to cool.
When cold, transfer the contents of the pan to a clean plastic / metal container and store in the fridge for 24 hours to allow the flavours to develop.
Then pass the stock through a fine sieve, discarding the vegetables.
This stock will keep refrigerated for up to 3 days or can be frozen for up to 4 months.

basic 7.

LOBSTER OR LANGOUSTINE CAPPUCCINO SAUCE

500ml langoustine / lobster stock - *see basic 1*
Pinch Cayenne pepper
1 teaspoon fresh lemon juice
1 clove garlic, finely sliced
200ml double cream

Add all the ingredients to the saucepan and simmer for 15 minutes.
Pass through a sieve and set aside until ready to use.

basic 8.

CHICKEN JUS

1½kg fresh chicken wings, chopped into 3cm pieces
50g unsalted butter
1 carrot, peeled and cut into 2cm dice
2 sticks celery, cut into 2cm dice
1 onion, peeled and cut into 2cm dice
100ml dry white wine
100ml Madeira
500ml fresh chicken stock - *see basic 3*
300ml fresh veal stock - *see basic 4*
1 tomato, chopped
1 clove garlic, peeled and sliced
4 sprigs fresh tarragon

Fry the wings in vegetable oil in a pan on the stove until they are golden brown.
Remove the wings from the pan and drain off the excess oil.
Add the butter to the pan along with the chopped vegetables and sauté them until they are golden brown.
Add the white wine to the vegetables and reduce it to a glaze.
Put the chicken wings back into the pan and pour in the Madeira.
Reduce the liquid by two thirds volume and add the stocks, tomato and garlic.
Bring the sauce to the boil and cook rapidly for 15-20 minutes or until reduced by two thirds volume.
Remove the pan from the heat, add the tarragon and allow it to rest for 20 minutes.
Strain the sauce through a fine sieve.

basic 9.

MUSHROOM AND ROSEMARY JUS

200ml fish stock - *see basic 2*
400ml chicken stock - *see basic 3*
400ml veal stock - *see basic 4*
500g button mushrooms, sliced
3 cloves garlic, peeled and sliced
1 sprig rosemary

Place all the ingredients in a pan, except for the rosemary, and reduce to 400ml liquid.
Add the rosemary to the sauce. Allow to cool, then strain.

basic 10.
WHITE WINE VELOUTÉ

50g unsalted butter
2 shallots, finely sliced
200ml white wine
250ml chicken stock - *see basic 3*
250ml double cream

Melt the butter in a saucepan and gently sweat the shallots for 1 minute without colouring.
Add the white wine and reduce to a glaze.
Add the chicken stock and reduce to 300ml.
Add the double cream and bring the sauce to the boil for 2 minutes.
Pass through a fine sieve, season with a little salt.

basic 11.
BEURRE BLANC

120ml dry white wine
1 tablespoon white wine vinegar
1 shallot, finely chopped
5 white peppercorns, crushed
6 tablespoons double cream
200g unsalted butter, cold and diced
½ lemon
Salt

Bring the white wine, vinegar, shallot and white peppercorns to the boil and reduce by half.
Add the double cream and boil for one minute.
Lower the heat and gradually whisk in the cold diced butter, add a squeeze of lemon juice and check the seasoning.
Pass through a fine sieve into a clean pan, gently warm but do not boil, as this will separate the sauce.

basic 12.
LEMON GRASS CAPPUCCINO

2 shallots, finely sliced
3 stalks lemon grass, bruised and sliced finely
350ml white wine
350ml fish stock - *see basic 2*
300ml double cream
Salt

Place the shallots, lemon grass and white wine in a saucepan and cook until almost all the liquid is absorbed.
Add the fish stock and reduce by two thirds.
Add the cream and return to the boil, then remove from the heat.
Adjust the seasoning and strain through a fine sieve.

basic 13.

FRESH PASTA

(makes 500g)

2 whole eggs
4 egg yolks
450g plain or '00' pasta flour
Pinch salt
3 tablespoon cold water
1 tablespoon olive oil

Crack the whole eggs into a bowl with the egg yolks and beat together with a whisk. Set aside.
Put the flour and salt into an electric mixer bowl or food processor and mix on a very low speed.
Slowly add the eggs and beat to a smooth dough.
Add the water and olive oil, turn up the speed of the machine slightly and beat until the dough becomes smooth and even. This should only take about 2 –3 minutes.
Divide into four even pieces, cling film and leave to rest in the fridge for at least 1 hour.

basic 14.

SPÄTZLE

500g plain flour
6 whole eggs (medium sized)
50g fromage frais
Pinch nutmeg
Pinch salt

Place all of the ingredients together into a large bowl and beat well to form a smooth paste.
Spoon a little of the mix onto a small chopping board and scrape thin horizontal lines into a pan of salted boiling water to form individual pieces approximately 3-5cm in length.
Allow the Spätzle to cook for 2 minutes then transfer to ice cold water to chill.
Drain the Spätzle once they are all cooked and place in a bowl until ready to re-heat.

basic 15.

BRAISED WHOLE LEEKS

50g unsalted butter
4 leeks, trimmed and washed (approx. 20cm long)
100ml Sauvignon Blanc white wine
350ml chicken stock - *see basic 3*
1 small bunch thyme
2 cloves garlic
Salt

Melt the butter in a large pan, cut the leeks in half and gently colour them until golden brown.
Pour in the white wine and reduce by two thirds by boiling rapidly.
Add the chicken stock, thyme, garlic and a couple pinches of salt.
Bring to the boil and cook on top of the stove until the liquid has reduced by half.
Transfer the pan to the oven and continue to braise until the leeks are tender and the stock has reduced to a glaze.
When cooked, leave them to cool and store in the reduced stock until ready to serve.

basic 16.

LEEK CREAM

600g leeks, dark leaves removed
75g unsalted butter
250ml chicken stock, hot - *see basic 3*
200ml double cream, hot
Salt

Slice the leeks very finely and wash well, then drain.
Melt the butter in a wide pan and add the leeks with a little salt.
Cook quickly until starting to soften.
Add the hot chicken stock and reduce until almost completely absorbed, then add the cream and boil for 2 minutes.
Place the pan contents into a blender and purée until smooth.
Adjust the seasoning with salt if necessary.

basic 17.

SHALLOT CREAM

200g shallots, peeled and finely sliced
200g onion, peeled and finely sliced
100g unsalted butter

Cook the shallots and onion gently in the butter without colouring for 5 minutes.
Add one tablespoon of water and cover with greaseproof paper.
Cook for a further 20 minutes on a low heat until soft. (If required add an additional tablespoon of water)
Transfer the contents of the pan into a liquidiser and purée until smooth.
Adjust the seasoning with salt if required.

basic 18.

BRAISED SAVOY CABBAGE

1 whole Savoy cabbage
2 medium sized carrots
1 onion, peeled and finely sliced
150g good quality smoked bacon
50g duck fat or lard
2 sprigs fresh thyme
2 cloves garlic
150ml dry white wine
250ml fresh chicken stock - *see basic 3*

Remove the tough outside cabbage leaves.
Cut the cabbage into quarters, discard the core and roughly shred the leaves.
Cut the carrots into long batons about 5mm thick.
Cut the bacon into lardons (strips).
In a heavy-based pan melt the duck fat and cook the bacon for 3 minutes.
Add the carrots and onions to the pan and cook for a further 2-3 minutes.
Add the white wine, chicken stock, thyme and garlic and bring it to the boil.
Add the cabbage, cover with greaseproof paper and cook in the oven at 200°C (Gas mark 6) for 15-20 minutes.

basic 19.

BRAISED FENNEL

1kg fennel bulbs
100ml extra virgin olive oil
200ml white wine
4 cloves garlic, peeled and halved
1 small bunch thyme
400ml fresh chicken stock - *see basic 3*

Cut the fennel into quarters lengthways.
Heat the olive oil in a pan and gently cook the fennel with a pinch of salt until golden brown on both cut sides.
Add the white wine, garlic and thyme to the pan.
Reduce the wine to a glaze then add the chicken stock and cover with a round of greaseproof paper (cartouche).
Place in a hot oven, 200°C (Gas mark 6) for 15-20 minutes until the vegetables are cooked through and the stock has reduced to a glaze.
Allow the fennel to cool in the liquid.
Re-heat the fennel in the stock when required.

basic 20.

CITRUS FENNEL

1 bulb fennel, peeled and finely sliced
1 star anise
Vegetable stock (nage) to cover - *see basic 6*
2 cloves garlic, peeled and halved
40g unsalted butter
Juice ½ lemon
Salt

Put all of the ingredients except the lemon juice into a wide pan.
Bring the liquid up to the boil and cook it rapidly until the liquid is well reduced and the fennel is just cooked.
Stir in the lemon juice to taste.
Cover and keep warm until required.

basic 21.

CAULIFLOWER PURÉE

250g cauliflower florets, stalks removed
70g unsalted butter
450ml milk
Pinch salt

Slice the cauliflower florets as finely as you possibly can and set them aside.
Melt the butter in a wide-based pan over a low heat.
Add the cauliflower with a pinch of salt and 3 tablespoons of water and cook without colouring for 3 minutes.
Add half of the milk, turn up the heat and simmer until the liquid is well reduced.
Add the rest of the milk and cook until the liquid has reduced, but enough remains to form a loose purée. The cauliflower should be cooked and soft.
Transfer to a blender and purée until smooth.

basic 22.

CELERIAC PURÉE

1 medium sized celeriac
150ml double cream
50g unsalted butter

Trim and peel the celeriac and cut into large even sized pieces.
Cook in boiling salted water until tender. Drain and steam off any excess moisture.
Add the double cream and simmer until reduced by half.
Purée in a liquidiser and add the butter.
When smooth, remove and hang in a muslin bag to remove any further moisture.
This should have a consistency to be able to hold its shape, for example to be able to form a quenelle using 2 spoons.

basic 23.

SPINACH WITH LEMON

225g baby spinach, washed and dried
50ml olive oil
1 lemon or lime
1 clove garlic

Heat the olive oil in a large pan until it is very hot.
Add the spinach, cook for 30 seconds stirring all the time with a wooden spoon.
When cooked, add just a few slices of fresh garlic and let it infuse in the pan off the heat with a lid on.
Add the juice of a whole lemon or lime.
Sprinkle with salt.

basic 24.

HOLLANDAISE SAUCE

30ml white wine vinegar
1 small shallot, sliced
1 sprig tarragon
10 white peppercorns
2 egg yolks
250ml clarified butter at 32-40°C (*butter that has been melted and had any solids or whey removed*)

In a saucepan bring the white wine vinegar, shallot, tarragon and peppercorns to the boil. Reduce by two thirds, then pour through a fine sieve and set aside.
Place the egg yolks in a large round stainless steel bowl.
Add the vinegar reduction and 1 tablespoon of water.
Place the bowl over a pan of boiling water and whisk vigorously until the mixture has doubled in quantity. This will take approximately 2-3 minutes.
Using a small ladle, slowly add the clarified butter, which should be between 32-40°C, to the egg yolks, whisking all the time.
When all the butter is added, season with a little salt and lemon juice, cover with cling film and store in a warm place, around 22-26°C.
This must be used within 1-2 hours.

basic 25.

TARRAGON VINAIGRETTE

300ml white wine vinegar
Salt, approx 1 tablespoon
2 sprigs tarragon
2 cloves garlic, peeled and sliced
1 litre extra virgin olive oil
700ml peanut oil
30 grinds white pepper

Warm the vinegar in a pan with the salt until dissolved.
Add the tarragon to the vinegar and pour into a large bowl.
Add the garlic, then the remaining ingredients, whisking to combine.
Bottle with the tarragon and garlic.
Keeps in the fridge for up to 12 weeks.

basic 26.

SWEET PASTRY

100g diced butter
300g plain flour
Pinch salt
90g icing sugar, sifted
1½ eggs, beaten

Cut the butter into small dice and soften to room temperature.
Sift the flour and salt onto a work surface and make a well in the centre.
Add the butter and sugar and gently work together with your fingertips until the texture resembles breadcrumbs.
Make a well in the centre and add the beaten eggs.
Gradually draw in the flour with your fingers until it has all been incorporated.
Form the dough into a ball, being careful not to over-work it.
Wrap the ball in cling film and refrigerate for at least 3 hours before use.

basic 27.

CRÈME CHANTILLY

200ml double cream
25g icing sugar
1 vanilla pod

Halve the vanilla pod and scrape out seeds into a small bowl.
Add the cream and icing sugar.
Whisk the cream until thick.

basic 28.

ALMOND ANGLAISE SAUCE

200ml milk
150ml double cream
5 egg yolks
80g sugar
100g flaked almonds

Pour the milk and cream into a saucepan.
Bring to the boil.
Whisk the sugar with the egg yolks until pale in colour.
Pour half of the boiled milk and cream over the egg mixture.
Mix together and then add back to the pan containing the other half of the milk and cream.
Place back onto a low heat, stirring all the time, until the sauce coats the back of a wooden spoon.
Take off the heat and pass though a sieve.
Place the flaked almonds onto an oven tray and bake in a hot oven at 190°C (Gas mark 5) for a few minutes until you obtain a good golden colour.
Add the almonds to the sauce and leave to cool.

Note: *You can serve the Anglaise warm or cold but do not allow it to boil as the eggs will scramble.*

basic 29.

LEMON ANGLAISE SAUCE

250ml double cream
250ml milk
Zest 2 lemons
5 egg yolks
100g caster sugar

Put the cream, milk and lemon zest into a heavy-based saucepan and bring to the boil.
Place the egg yolks and sugar into a large mixing bowl and whisk together well until pale in colour.
Whisk in half of the hot milk and cream and then add back to the pan containing the other half of the milk and cream.
Place the pan back onto the heat and cook on a low heat stirring continuously until the mixture coats the back of the spoon, and then transfer into a container to cool.

Note: *You can serve the Anglaise warm or cold but do not allow it to boil as the eggs will scramble.*

recipe index

DESSERTS

BASICS

“Thanks”

Firstly a special *thank you* to all my customers, without whom the restaurant would not exist.

Thank you to my loyal and creative management team: *Joe Taggart, Steven Spear, Rikki Preston, Bruce Rennie, Scott Ross, Steven Strachan* and to all the staff at the Restaurant and the Cook School.

Thank you also to all my previous staff *Paul, Craig, Jean-Christophe, Jose, Vivien, Arnaud, Salvatore* and so many more.

Our reputation relies on the freshest produce from our suppliers, so thank you to all of them.

Many I have worked with for over 10 years:

Darren and *Stevie* from Campbells Prime Meats.

Craig from Braehead foods.

Alistair from Clarks Speciality Foods.

Patricia from Phantassie Farm Organic Vegetables.

Ali from Capital Fruit and Vegetables.

Duncan from Strathspey Mushrooms.

J.B. and *Mark* from Mark Murphy.

Kenneth and *Alistair* from Villeneuve Wines.

Zubair from Raeburn Fine Wines.

Adrian from T.M. Robertson.

Tarquin from Inverarity Vaults.

Giles from Alliance Wines.

David Lowrie.

Iain Mellis.

Michel Roux for the training he gave me and his kind words.

Alan Donaldson for his mouth-watering photography - *just fantastic!*

Peter and *Jane McDermott*, *Scott Ross* and *Fiona Armstrong* for their enthusiasm, ideas and hard work developing this book.

Su Hesketh from Crimson Edge.

And of course my *Mum* and *Dad*, *Eric* and *Gary* for their constant support and help.